WALES

Edited by Lynsey Hawkins

First published in Great Britain in 2003 by
YOUNG WRITERS
Remus House,
Coltsfoot Drive,
Peterborough, PE2 9JX
Telephone (01733) 890066

HB ISBN 0 75434 253 0
SB ISBN 0 75434 254 9

FOREWORD

This year, the Young Writers' The Write Stuff! competition proudly presents a showcase of the best poetic talent from over 40,000 up-and-coming writers nationwide.

Young Writers was established in 1991 and we are still successful, even in today's modern world, in promoting and encouraging the reading and writing of poetry.

The thought, effort, imagination and hard work put into each poem impressed us all, and once again, the task of selecting poems was a difficult one, but nevertheless, an enjoyable experience.

We hope you are as pleased as we are with the final selection and that you and your family continue to be entertained with *The Write Stuff! Wales* for many years to come.

CONTENTS

Brecon High School

Charmaine Cunningham	87
Jason Holmes	87
Adelle Faulds	88
Holly Menzies	88
Thomas West	89
Calum Vaughan	89
Mark Butler	90
Craig Norman	90
Tom Jayne	91
Sam Richards	92
Luke Harris	92
Susy Stark	93
Laura Rice	93
Christina Watson	94
Robert Peacock	95
Hannah James	96
Luke Courtney-Hart	96
Rhys Dawe	97
Francis Tomlins	97
Mari Davies	98
Lotti Jones	99
Robyn Taylor	100
Teresa Bruton	100
Ellie Deering	101
Lucy Blowfield	102
Rory Wesson	103
James Woods	104
Stacey Price	104
Dale Williams	105
Giselle Quarrington	106
Benjamin Townley	106
Nathan Collins	107
Owen West	107
Emily Wright	108
Kim Brown	109
Callie Jones	110
Bridie Horler	110
Daniel Goodall	111

Llandrindod High School

Naomi Sullivan	189
David Ramplee	189
Shane Healey	190
Liam Robinson	190
Ben Griffiths	191
Karl Harris	192
Aaron Martin	192
Matthew Baynham	193
Sarah Woodward	193
Nathan Davies	194
Rachel Williams	194
Gwneda Wozencraft	195
Lauren Morgan	195
Heidi Harries	196
Kirsty Doman	196
Sophie Williams	197
Adam Stephens	198
Thomas Simmons	198
Kyle King	199
Danielle Cosgrave	199
Russell Thomas	200
Vikki Young	200
Stuart Eyre	201
Nerys Hammond	202
Hannah Lloyd	202
David Pritchard	203
Ieuan Hughes	204
Owne Major	204
Chloe Davis	205
Emma Davies	206
Sam Glenton	206
Craig Rees	207
Alyson Eyval	207

Penglais Comprehensive School

Rogrigo Buanafina	208
Helen Welsh	209
Steven Moss	209

The Poems

WHAT IS LIFE IF IT WASN'T FOR LOVE?

That stuff that keeps us searching,
never finding,
we think we know, but do we?
Have you found it?
Thought you had, but realised it was a fantasy,
not real,
not wanted,
not careful,
because care,
is the one thing we have to protect ourselves,
to stop when we get too far,
to turn back if we're scared,
when we find love we lose something,
we lose care,
who cares?
You're in love,
really?
Not just a miracle?
Never sure, are you?
Do you want to live in a world with real love
coming once in a blue moon,
or -
in a world where love is always around you?
You know,
you feel it,
but do you lose your care?
Not in that world,
that world is perfect,
too perfect,
if there is only love and no hate,
the love seems normal,
nothing special,
with hatred to counterbalance the love in our world, we need this love,
without it, our world would mean nothing,

without it,
hate would feel normal,
hate would be around us constantly,
without love that hate is nothing
without hate,
love doesn't exist.
Think!
What do you want?
always love
or a special love,
a love you can only have one chance with?
You decide
then you can tell me if you want to be loved by everyone,
always?
Yes?
No?
Me!
I'd prefer the chance to be in love once and experience it fully
in a world with hate,
because in a world with hate, the love is more real,
more needed.
Tell me which would you prefer?

Bonnie Phillips (16)

ME

My mum's on a diet, my dad's on the booze,
My gran's out playing bingo, but she was born to lose.
My brother stripped his motorbike, although it's bound to rain,
My sister's playing Elton John, over and over *again!*

What a dim old family, what a dreadful lot,
Sometimes I think I'm the only superstar they've got!

Joanna Walters (11)

NURSERY RHYMES

N ursery rhymes can be fun
U nderstood by everyone
R hyming little ditties
S aid in towns and cities
E very child should know one
R ead to them by their mum
Y et no matter how old.

R hymes are always told
H ere, there and everywhere
Y es something that we all can share
M ums and dads, old folks too
E veryone including you
S ay a nursery rhyme!

Andrew Evans (12)
Blackwood Comprehensive School

WHO IS IT?

If she were an animal she would be a horse,
If she were a musical instrument she would be a drum,
If she were a building she would be a shed.
If she were a plant she would be a dead daisy.
If she were food, she would be a carrot.
If she were a drink, she would be a lemonade.
Her colour is white,
Her season is winter.
Her time of night is midnight,
She is a weapon, she is a gun,
She is a car, an old banger car!

Stephen Nutt (13)
Blackwood Comprehensive School

HELL

A forest of fire
An ocean of lava
A sky of blood
A beach of oblivion
A castle of creatures
A mansion of mayhem
A dungeon of doom
A house of horror
A gateway to evil's afterlife.

Hell
!
Not as good as Heaven
Not as bad as Uncle Will singing
Down here, you don't hear bells ringing
Love is forbidden, hate is required
To fulfil what the master desires
Souls are found roaming around
Heads are chopped off and placed on the gate
They are just thrown around and ate
Fingers and toes are fed to the master.
If not, it would be a disaster.
Hell screams and shouts at souls roaming about
Hang them on the wall, not let them off at all
Beat them, bash them, whip them and lock them.

Kieron Brown (12)
Blackwood Comprehensive School

THE BIG CON

Brontosaurus, stegosaurus, whatever the name;
Tyrannosaurus, spinosaurus, it's one and the same -
They clubbed together, one and all
To make the rest of us all look small!

As long as a cricket pitch, snout to tail
With tree trunk legs and plated mail.
Snarling like thunder and humped like a hill,
They could eat a whole haystack and be hungry still.

Alyn Nelson (13)
Blackwood Comprehensive School

LIFE /DEATH

Life/Living

Life and living
Right now I don't know what life is
It can be good,
It can be bad
And sometimes, it can be senseless.
But I know this -
We must treasure our life
With all our heart.

Death/Dying

Death and dying
No one knows what death feels like
No one knows what happens after you die.
People are afraid of dying.
People die, every day.
How do you want to die?
Asleep or awake!
Think about it
Before it happens!

Gareth Mark Pope (12)
Blackwood Comprehensive School

UNTITLED

If he was a building he would
be a skyscraper,
If he was an animal he would
be a gorilla,
If he was a plant he would
be a thorn bush.
If he was a chocolate bar he would
be a Yorkie bar,
If he was a car he would be a monster truck.
If he was a drink he would be a
bottle of Lucozade,
His best time of the year
is Boxing Day,
His favourite colour is red.
If he were a country he would be America.
He is Lennox Lewis.

Scott Giles (13)
Blackwood Comprehensive School

THE TORNADO

The tornado was faster than lightning
It was very, very frightening
And it was also exciting
All night it kept fighting.

It scared all the tiny animals
All of the animals went wiry,
Then the tornado went fiery
And I wrote it in my diary.

Then the tornado left New York . . .

Daniel Spencer (14)
Blackwood Comprehensive School

CHRISTMAS

Don't drink and drive at Christmas
it's just a stupid thing
if you drink and drive at Christmas
you might hit a reindeer thing

Santa rides in his sleigh
and you ride in a car.
So if Santa gives you coal
don't hit him with your car.

Rudolph has a red nose
he doesn't drink and fly
so why should you in your car
try to drink and drive?

Jack Gore (13)
Blackwood Comprehensive School

LOVE POEM

Your eyes are as blue as the sea
Your hair is as soft as silk
You are as thin as a model walking
down the catwalk.
Your skin is the colour of a peach and
as soft as one too.
Your lips are as red as a red pen and your
voice is as soft as a whisper in the wind.
You're witty and smart, just how
I like you.
So please would you
go out with me?

Simon Tudball (13)
Blackwood Comprehensive School

My School Day

My alarm goes off, screeching in my ear,
Got to get up, the morning time is here.

I go into the bathroom, clean my teeth and wash my face,
I put in my bag, all my books and my pencil case.

I get into my uniform, dressed smart from head to toe,
I put up my hair, and then I'm ready to go.

I arrive at school, just before the bell,
Feet start moving, children start to yell.

The teacher takes the register, names called one by one,
Soon tutorial is over and off to the first lesson we run.

I sit through my first two lessons, trying to stay awake,
Then all of a sudden the bell rings. Great! It's time for break.

I sit in the canteen with all my friends, having a little snack,
Laughing and giggling with all my mates, but in no time
we have to go back.

I sit through my third and fourth lessons, waiting for quarter past one,
My stomach rumbling and making noises, oh when will dinner
time come!

The afternoon whizzes by, one lesson and we're done,
Yes! It's home time, enough school, off home to have some fun.

Sarah Carys Rogers (13)
Blackwood Comprehensive School

Wales

Oh how I love our country of Wales
To climb up and run down vales.
To listen to the old Celtic tales
Oh how I love our country of Wales.

To be called Welsh, makes me very proud.
I sing our Anthem extremely loud.
In rugby shirt and leek when St David's Day comes around,
To be called Welsh, makes me very proud.

Nicole Hurley (13)
Blackwood Comprehensive School

FEELINGS/THE WAY I AM

Sometimes I feel happy and glad
And at times I feel sad.
Sometimes I'm good and
Sometimes I'm bad.
But other times I feel disappointed,
Depressed, let down and stressed out.
But this I know, I'm not perfect
And I'm certainly not the best.
But when the day comes when I feel good about myself
Will be the day I can rest.
Knowing I'm top of the range
And feel no pain.
How you feel about yourself inside is what really counts
And how you feel can sometimes feel like a roller coaster ride.
As how you feel is who you are
And knowing who you are is the best thing in life
And you know what they say . . .
. . . the best things in life are free!
This is one of the best things in life
which is completely free!

Sam Thomas (13)
Blackwood Comprehensive School

IT HAD ALL BEEN A DREAM, OR WAS IT?

One dark, wet and foggy night,
Something caught my line of sight.
Standing in this eerie wood,
Stood something under a cloak and hood.

'Hello there!' I did bellow and shout,
But no words did it call out.
I walked towards this voiceless thing,
But stopped in my tracks as it started to sing.

I blinked for a second and then it was gone,
Now behind me, it was wailing its song.
Not much more of it could I stand,
As my gun was slipping from my hand.

I never stopped to wonder why,
But raised the rifle to my eye.
I wished I were home, safe in my bed
Not here, facing this instead.

And then I woke up
All covered in sweat,
It had all been a dream,
Or had it?

Helen Eynon (14)
Blackwood Comprehensive School

FOOTBALL

Football's crazy, football's mad,
Football's happy, football's sad!
Football is a popular sport,
It's all you see in the Sunday paper report.

In football you get fouled,
If the ref messed up, everybody howled.
Yes, football is the beautiful game,
This is one sport that is not lame!

Matthew Phillpott (13)
Blackwood Comprehensive School

SEASONS

Howling and prowling,
Rustling the trees,
Watching and waiting
Creating a breeze.

Smashing and splitting
As it hits the ground,
Dampening and drowning,
Travelling around.

Scorching and sizzling
One hundred degrees,
Burning and baking,
Evaporating the seas.

Freezing and frosting,
Everything it touches.
Decorating and dazzling,
The world at its clutches.

Equal and exciting
Are the seasons,
Luxurious and lovely,
Don't need any reasons.

Cerys Davies (13)
Blackwood Comprehensive School

WHO'S AFRAID OF THE BIG BAD WOLF?

Who's afraid of the big bad wolf
With his eerie howl and his dripping fangs?
Or who's not afraid of the big bad wolf
Who thinks they're cuddly things?
Who thinks they'd rather rip your arm off, than
be embraced with a hug?
Who thinks under that rough and unloved exterior
there's a lovely little teddy bear?
Who thinks they're wild, killing machines,
and who doesn't?
Why do we fear the big, bad wolf?
Do they deserve such a bad reputation?
Decide quickly,
So I ask you again
Who's afraid of the big bad wolf?
Many people it seems, but I ask you this -
How many of you have ever met a wild wolf?
Yet you still fear the creature who prowls around at night
with its gleaming yellow eyes, softly padding feet and
just audible snarl, now and then.
So now are you afraid of the big bad wolf?
You'd better be!

Sarah Blackwell (13)
Blackwood Comprehensive School

CATZ

In the deep shadows of the night
The cat's green eyes are bright
Against the glowing moonlight
Its dark black body stirs through
The freshly mown lawns

Just waiting for the arrival of dawn
Its curly black tail sways about the trees,
Knocking dewdrops to the ground.
Yet still a sound cannot be found
In the darkness of the night.

Rebecca McDonald (13)
Blackwood Comprehensive School

DISCO

Oh no! What shall I wear?
I've got a zit, it's so unfair!
It's big and bright red on the end of my nose,
I look like Rudolph, a freak, I suppose.

I've found a top to wear, although it's a bit small,
I've got these really high heels; I'm bound to fall.
I have a pair of trousers and they are quite cool,
I'm only joking, I look like a fool.

My lipstick's all smudged,
My blackened eyelashes will not budge!
It gets worse as if this wasn't bad enough,
My mother is driving me in her old banger, I said I'd walk.
She said, 'Tough!'

I knew I'd trip and fall on the floor!
I ended up at casualty's door
Despite all of this, one thing's really cool
I've broken my leg, so I can't go to school!

Ellen Rowe (13)
Blackwood Comprehensive School

SPORT

There're many, many sports
of all different sorts.

There's netball, football and a mile long run,
which for some can be agonising and others
so much fun.

Some sports are fast and some are slow,
some backwards, some forwards, do you go.

Some sports use nets or posts and balls
some can be no contact and others all falls.

There're many, many sports
of all different sorts.

Emma Prosser (13)
Blackwood Comprehensive School

ICE T

If he was an animal he would be a smoky bear,
If he was an instrument he would be a thumping drum,
If he was a building he would be an ice-cold mansion.
If he was a plant he would be a hemp plant.
If he was a food he would be a chilli con carne.
If he was a drink he would be a cup of iced tea.
His colour is brown
His season is summer
His time of day is 9.17pm.
If he was a weapon, he would be a tommy gun.
If he was as car, he would be a Lotus Elise.
He is Ice T.

Mark Thomas (13)
Blackwood Comprehensive School

THE SALE

Been searching through the catalogue all day
Waiting to see what's going to be at the big sale.
All sound perfect in their own little way
Seen the one I want, she's a beautiful bay.

The big day has come!
I check the lot number, trying to find the mare,
I get to the pen and it's completely bare
I ask somewhere where she is
But nobody seems to care.

I just want to see if she's good, bad, all's correct,
If she's what I'm looking for.
I've just got to pray she's the one I get.

Kristina Jones (13)
Blackwood Comprehensive School

WHO IS HE?

If he was an animal he would be a fun lovin' pup.
If he was a musical instrument he would be a rock 'n' roll drum.
If he was a building he would be a strip club.
If he was a plant he would be a Venus flytrap.
If he was a food he would be stringy food like spaghetti.
If he was a drink he would be a sharp, sour drink.
His season is the mating season.
His time of day is club time.
He is a sniper's gun.

Sean Morgan (13)
Blackwood Comprehensive School

SAILING

The waves beat against the ship
gently rocking it.
The wind blows against the sails
making a steady whisper.

The salt in air burns but the
sea breeze makes it cooler.
There is no feeling here except for
the pleasure of being afloat.

The sounds you get used to
like the squeaking of the lifeboats
And the fluttering of the sails,
they are all things you can remember.

After a while you feel at home
as if you were on there all your life.
But you know you're only -
Sailing.

Lloyd Hambridge (13)
Blackwood Comprehensive School

LEAVES

Rain is falling
Leaves are floating
About the blowing wind
They change colour
And fall in the autumn
And they get carried away
On the rustling wind.

Liam Price (12)
Blackwood Comprehensive School

DEATH

Speed is like a drug,
If you do it once
You will do it again.

The thrills and spills
Are exciting
But still speed equals *me!*

Even though you missed
Me this time
I will catch you up.

This will be the last time
In which I ask -
Stop speeding!

Daniel Jefferies (13)
Blackwood Comprehensive School

THE SEA

Thrashing and smashing against the rocks
It bounces off piers
And throws ships off course
You never see a calm sea
Except in summertime
But then it still moves
Just back and forth
But never still
Just swishing and swaying
Shimmering in the sun
And gloomy in the rain.

Harriet Lewis (13)
Blackwood Comprehensive School

WHAT'S THAT ON MY NOSE?

I woke up one morning eager and bright,
then looked in the mirror to have a big fright.
There was my enemy perched on my nose,
making me shiver from my head to my toes.
I can't believe that it's happened to me,
there is no way in the world the people won't see.
Why did I wake up and look this way?
Why didn't this happen another day?
It's huge, it's enormous, the biggest I've seen,
it's ugly, disgusting, ferocious and mean.
What would people think and say?
All I could do was hope and pray.
No bathroom product could be used to hide -
this thing on my nose, so long and wide.
The day of the disco, the day of the dance
It might be unnoticed - hey I have no chance!
The most annoying thing is, I just can't see -
Why this big zit on my nose had landed on
          Me!

Kathryn Maguire (13)
Blackwood Comprehensive School

ACROSTIC POEM

A   time when leaves fall from the trees,
U   p in the air they blow everywhere.
T   he time to prepare for the freezing weather.
U   ntil next year when the weather gets better,
M   oving trees gives us the clues,
N   ow autumn is here with colourful views.

Craig Harrhy (12)
Blackwood Comprehensive School

THE DAY

I wake up in the morning,
The day is miserable,
The day is lazy.
I get out of bed,
I get out of my door,
I rush downstairs for my clothes,
I leave the house for school,
I can feel the rain coming through my shoes,
I get to school,
I get indoors looking at the rain,
Saying the day is miserable.
The day is lazy but it must go on.
I'm looking ahead,
It's still raining and I keep saying
The day is miserable,
The day is lazy,
But the day must go on.
The day, the day.

Daniel Burgess (12)
Blackwood Comprehensive School

SPEED

Don't kill a child
Just kill your speed
Driving too fast - there is no need.
So please drive slowly
You know it makes sense
Because to kill a child is a
Criminal offence.

Katie Hamer (12)
Blackwood Comprehensive School

THAT ALIEN STOLE MY TEACHER!

Another boring assembly
All gathered in the hall
When Mr Pickard introduces the guest
The children's voices all stall.

'This is Zonk,' he clearly says
Whilst wiping his nose with glee.
'He has a proposition for us
Which he is sure you will agree.'

'Hello everybody,' said Zonk,
'I have delightful news . . .'
And in a giant puff of smoke
He vaporised Miss Cruwys.

Teacher after teacher disappeared
Without a second of doubt
And there goes Mr Gregg
Then one boy stands up and shouts . . .

'That's my teacher, you stupid alien,
Now bloomin' put him back,
He'll be angry when he gets out
And he'll throw you straight out. *Smack!'*

All the children gasped with disbelief,
'He must have lost his mind!'
As Zonk floats quickly down the causeway
With the staff not far behind.

Daniel Lewis (13)
Blackwood Comprehensive School

BIRDS

The birds flutter their pretty wings,
They sing their own beautiful song.
They sing it all day long,
They're busy doing things
That only birds do.
Making nests and feeding their young.

They preen their feathers,
Trying to survive in all weathers.
The ground so hard and dry,
What a treat . . .
We can now see them fly.

Soaring so high,
Enjoying their flight.
So graceful, so elegant,
Gliding high and diving low.
A beautiful sight,
Let's watch them go.

Their beaks so strong,
Their feathers so fine
They chirp so sweetly
All the time.

They sing their special dawn chorus,
Especially for us.

Rachel Ann Andrews (13)
Blackwood Comprehensive School

TEACHERS!

Teachers only give you homework
And they like to scream and shout,
Write, write, write - is all they think about.
English, maths, science and Welsh
These subjects are just so boring.

I really hate learning, there's
Too much to remember.
All I really want to do
Is go out with my friends.

So many pencils and pens,
And different pieces of paper.
Letters in different shapes and sizes,
All over the page, but still no work is done.

Teachers just talk all the lesson, and
You don't get any work done.
And it's always your fault,
If it never gets completed.

Kady Edwards (13)
Blackwood Comprehensive School

HOMEWORK

H   omework Miss?
O   h, I was away
M   e? I forgot
E   veryone's forgotten have they?
W   hat Miss?
O   h!
R   ight!
K   eeping us behind!

Robert Wilson (13)
Blackwood Comprehensive School

GOLF IS A NIGHTMARE

Golf is hard, choosing the right club.
On the windy, birdie par.
The accuracy of the shot counted on this shot.
This time there's water on this course
with a dog leg too.
There are people shouting *'Four!'* All the time
and frightening the living daylights out of everyone.
Then everyone ducks, just in case the ball hits you.
I think it's quite funny.

This putt is crucial, another two shots
and it will be over par.
I take the shot, it goes in - hooray!
I'm one under par.

David Ridout (12)
Blackwood Comprehensive School

LOVE IS GREAT

L   ove is something that should not be messed with
O   f course love is good, it's
V   ery cool. You always know when it is.
E   very person has love some time in their life.

I   think love is great
S   o it's really good.

G   ood love is always the best but
R   eal love is the warmest,
E   at your heart out if it's bad
A   ctive love is quite cool
T   o end this all, keep it good.

Matthew Taylor (13)
Blackwood Comprehensive School

SEASONS

Summer is when it starts to get hotter,
People are having fun.
The sun is shining brightly in the sky,
Everyone loves the sun.

Autumn is when the leaves fall,
The days get shorter.
In autumn, the sky gets dark quickly
And it gets colder.

Winter is when the weather gets bad,
We love it when it snows.
On the roads it gets really icy
And we get a red nose.

Spring is when the flowers bloom
The lambs are about.
The weather is getting better
There are flowers out.

Leanne Rutterford (13)
Blackwood Comprehensive School

SCARED

S   cared, that's what I am
C   uddled up like a little lamb
A   s a shadow creeps on to my bed
R   easons running through my head
E   erie ghosts and one-eyed ghouls
D   eadly monsters holding tools!

Adam Hughes (14)
Blackwood Comprehensive School

THE BIG ONE!

I'm running through a field
The sun is on me, can't run anymore,
Looking for a way to get through,
The sun shining so brightly on my face.
Dodging people as I run through.
People looking at me, shouting my name,
My tongue has gone dry,
I think I'm going to collapse,
No! I have to keep running,
I look up, I'm near the end.
I'm wondering what place I will come,
Running through to the finish line.
Twelfth.

Danielle Smith (12)
Blackwood Comprehensive School

KITE!

The kite flying in the sky
Gliding, gliding way up high
Twisting and turning
Swirling and swerving

Its bright colours shine off the sun
Filling young children full of fun
This kite, what a brilliant thing
Passing cloud, breeze and bird wing!

Josie Nabialek (13)
Blackwood Comprehensive School

MOTORBIKE

I clean, wash and tune up my KTM,
It's a 250,
I ride up and down the field,
I turn the throttle and the gears,
I spin around the corners,
I stop and start, lap after lap,
I turn around the corner to my house,
I have a race tomorrow.

The next day the weather is cold and foggy
And we get ready on the starting line,
We all set off,
Corner after corner, lap after lap,
I'm in third place,
We look at each other in anger to see who wins,
Last corner, brake and *crash!*

Ross Cornwell (12)
Blackwood Comprehensive School

I HATE YOU

Your eyes are as red as a monkey's bum,
Your hair is as orange as a baboon's feet.
Your body is like a shrivelled up prune.
Your skin is like puffed up fish,
Your lips are as green as a gone-off tomato.
Your voice is as mannish as a rhino.
Your personality is like a dummy, sucking its thumb.

Richard Howard (13)
Blackwood Comprehensive School

FRIENDS

Without a friend, what would I be?
No one to talk to and no one to see.
Alone and unhappy I would be sitting in my room
Wishing the phone would ring very soon.

We can tell our friends our secret thoughts,
Talk to them when we're sad,
They'll always be there for us
Whether we're good or bad.

A friendship lasts forever
Although we may be apart.
We'll always be remembered
Right from the very start.

Gemma Aubrey (13)
Blackwood Comprehensive School

THE BEACH

The sun shimmers onto the deep sea water
Reflecting into your eyes.
You can stand in the heat and feel the sand
Crunch beneath your feet.
The waves come crashing down.
They are big enough to knock you down.
The tide goes in and out
Like a snake slithering back and forth.

Alun Davies 13)
Blackwood Comprehensive School

SCHOOL

School,
You love it or you don't,
All the teachers moan.
Monday to Friday,
6 hours and 45 minutes a day,
The most boring lessons,
Geography, science, technology,
Give us a break,
Here comes dinner time,
Yeah, we're free,
For a while.
Last lesson drags as normal,
Here's the bell, we're
Free!

Katherine Jane Jones (12)
Blackwood Comprehensive School

THE BELL

Me, me and everyone else,
All waiting for the bell to ring,
1 minute, a few seconds,
Yes, the bell goes.
We all run out of the classroom
Like raging gorillas,
Running out of the school gates,
Getting ready for the bus.

Jade Louise Hamer (12)
Blackwood Comprehensive School

THE DOG NEXT DOOR

The dog next door just sits there all day
without a worry in the world.
His eyes are as black as night
with a little star beaming inside.
His coat is scruffy and is caked in mud,
He does not seem to care,
He smells of dog breath and mud.
I hear him breathing heavily,
looking around the garden.
I stroke him, the texture of his fur
feels like an old rag doll.
The dog next door is gentle and kind.
If only I was a dog.

Aimee Meredith (12)
Blackwood Comprehensive School

SCHOOL'S OUT!

It's the last day of school,
I am sitting in my chair looking up and down,
My hand is hurting because I have done so much work,
My pencil is broken, my pen has run out,
It will be over soon, I hope.
10, 9, 8, 7, 6, 5, 4, 3, 2, 1. Yes.
'School is out!' someone cries,
We grab our bags and run out of the door,
A boy gets trampled, I get squashed,
A school day is over, time to go home,
But school's not over yet, there's still homework!

Ryan Griffiths (12)
Blackwood Comprehensive School

THE FINALS

I am standing here again in the wet, soggy mud,
We stand behind the safety bars,
Then, hear the roaring engine from a distance,
Then it sounds louder and louder to me until
The rally car rips around the corner,
Tearing apart the track behind it.
The feel of mud splattering against my face,
The smell of burning oil drifting up my nose,
The white smoke explodes from the exhaust pipes
Into my face, making me choke.
The taste of petrol makes me tremble,
They only come around the track once.

Alex Organ (12)
Blackwood Comprehensive School

HOMEWORK

It's the day when my homework gets handed in,
But I've forgotten it, maybe I can say it got chucked in the bin.
Maybe she'll give me another sheet,
Or maybe I'll be dead meat!
Last lesson comes, oh no,
Where shall I go?
Over here or over there,
Anywhere it's safe to stand and stare.
She asks me, I say it got chucked in the bin,
I ask for another sheet,
I was right, I am dead meat!

Niketa Booth (12)
Blackwood Comprehensive School

MY CR80 RACE

I polish my bike -
I put on my gear, 5 minutes to the race,
I'm going to the start line ready to race,
But there's something wrong with my brakes,
Oh well, better than not even starting,
We are revving our bikes now,
The second flag goes up,
The gates drop, I get out first,
But there's a big turning ahead!
I can't stop,
I try to use my gears to slow, but I'm going to crash,
I wake up in hospital with a fractured leg,
I don't think I'll be doing that again.

Ben Jones (12)
Blackwood Comprehensive School

GIRLS' CHANGING ROOM

I walk in, clothes everywhere,
Socks on the bench,
Shirt on the window sill,
There are clothes everywhere,
It is a complete mess,
It stinks as well of sweat,
When the girls run in and out.
The girls are coming, I'd better hide,
I hide in the cupboard,
I wait for them to go,
I then fall asleep.

James Freeman (13)
Blackwood Comprehensive School

PLEASE MISS!

'Please can I go home, Miss, can I go home for tea?'
'No you can't, you cheeky boy.'
That's what Miss said to me.
'Miss, can we paint please?' Joe asked gracefully.
'No you can't, you bad, bad girl.'
That's what Miss said to me.
Then poor Jack Jones, with face of fright, gulped and said,
'Please Miss, can we read, Miss?'
And with one bite snapped off his head,
Jack knew that he was dead.

'Let that be a warning to you all,
Never trust teachers, none at all!'

Lauren Powell (13)
Blackwood Comprehensive School

GHOSTS

G   hostly, gruesome, grisly, gory,
H   orrendous, hideous,
O   gres,
S   hocking, supernatural,
T   errifying, terrible,
S   pooky spirits.

Ross Goslin (13)
Blackwood Comprehensive School

SCHOOL

They say school is the best time of your life,
But sometimes I find it's nothing but strife,
English and biology I think are fine,
Maths and science a bit of a crime.
When I grow up and become someone's wife,
I'll agree with them school was the best time of my life.

Jodie Lee Shankland (13)
Blackwood Comprehensive School

MY WISH

If only

If only school was a fun place to be,
If only the world was made out of sweets
that I could eat all day long,
If only cartoon people were real
so that the world would be a comic place,
If only ruby-like sun would shine all year long.
If only . . . if only . . . it will never happen.

I wish

I wish that I could fly right up to the sky
I wish that learning was easy
I wish that teachers would stop blaming me
I wish . . . I wish . . . it will never happen.

Wishing cannot get you far,
Not even up to a star.

But life is so unfair,
You cannot live without a care.

Lee Bevan (12)
Brecon High School

I WISH...

I wish that all the food you liked was good for you,
and you could eat as much of it as you liked.
I wish that everyone was equal,
and no one was 'above' or 'below' anyone else.
I wish that everyone would be kind,
and no one would be bullied.
I wish the whole world would help each other,
and no one would hate each other.
I wish that everyone was like a free spirit,
and didn't care about others' judgement of them.
I wish there was no fighting and war,
and everyone wanted peace.
I wish that friends were forever,
and that they would never forget me,
I wish that the homeless had homes,
and were happy and comfortable and warm.
I wish no one went hungry,
and everyone had a good quality of life.
I wish people listened,
instead of ignoring.
I wish all of this,
all this and more.

Emma Jones (12)
Brecon High School

GREEN

A springtime feeling,
A sack of grass,
The shamrock of Ireland,
Makes me think of the past.

A warm, inviting colour,
Over a dark row of trees,
In my garden I see,
The grass blowing in the breeze.

Caroline Galeozzie (11)
Brecon High School

MY DREAMS

Every darkness when the night comes,
My head fills with imagination and dreams,
Dreams unquestionable, unthinkable and unimaginable,
Nothing can stop me in this wave of dreams.

Dreams of battles of old,
Dreams of icy worlds so cold,
Dreams of events, future, present and past,
Dreams of never-ending sweets, they'll always last,
Dreams of great voyages at sea,
Dreams of places where no eye will see,
Dreams of great victories down at the ground,
Dreams of massive monsters with so much sound,
Dreams of amazing adventures in outer space,
Dreams of me going to a secret place.

So many to chose,
So many to lose,
In our brains,
Like a massive strain,
But what amazes me most,
Is how we're a host,
To a phenomenon that cannot be explained.

Lewis Owen (12)
Brecon High School

To Dream

If I could dream it would be to dream all year round,
I would dream to juggle with 5 clubs,
I would dream to swim on the ocean floor to see all the tropical fish,
I dream to ride a bike as fast as a comet,
I dream life is a long roller coaster,
I dream to sing like a professional,
I dream of flying roller coaster skates,
I dream of a warm spring day
And a cold winter's eve,
I dream to talk many languages,
I dream of successes in school,
I also dream of life on the moon,
Or to be an astronaut,
I dream that people were kind and not harsh,
But my favourite dream of all is not be a famous actor
But I love to dream all year round.

Sophie Rogers (12)
Brecon High School

If Only . . . .

If *only* school work was easy,
If *only* there was world peace,
If *only* Christmas was more often.
If *only* . . .

If *only* ill people could be cured,
If *only* there were six-legged chairs to swing on,
If *only* we did not have school uniform.
If *only* . . .

If *only* we could speak the languages of the world,
If *only* The Simpsons were real,
If *only* the secrets of the world were revealed
If *only* . . .

Robert Bussell (12)
Brecon High School

MONDAY

It hides behind Tuesday,
But it's one step ahead of Sunday,
It waits like a mantis,
Hungry for its prey.

The snakes wind up inside me,
Whilst it lies in wait,
Then the avalanche falls,
Then the mantis strikes,
Pounces like a tiger,
Because the time is right.

So what of it,
Now it's fed, does it go to sleep
Or lie in bed,
No this animal starts the game again,
For it has no boundaries,
No restrictions,
It goes by the name,
Monday.

Rowan Eves (12)
Brecon High School

HOPES AND DREAMS

I am just one person in this vast universe,
But my hopes and my dreams are important to me.

I dream of world peace where everyone is happy,
I hope for cures for diseases so everyone is healthy.

I dream of my dog and what life holds for her,
I hope for snow on Christmas Day every year.

I dream of becoming a vet, making creatures well,
I hope my aunty gets better and lives in peace.

I dream of a place where no one can hurt,
I hope to see the aurora lights shining brightly in the sky.

I am just one person in this vast universe,
My hopes and my dreams are important to me.

Genna Williams (13)
Brecon High School

MY DREAMS

To be a millionaire would be my dream come true,
To go to Disneyland and take a friend or two,
To go to Tenerife on holiday,
To meet all the stars for a day,
No more school to go to,
To meet the famous Man Utd,
To be famous is my dream,
To ride in a stretched limousine,
To meet my cousin who's two,
To read the thoughts of you,
I wish my dreams came true!

Claire Jones (12)
Brecon High School

FOLLOWER

I feel that something is following me,
It's going wherever I go.
It's still there when I walk to school,
It's hiding in a corner ready to strike,
Nobody else seems to see anything.

Will it follow me to my home?
What does it want with me?
It doesn't stop following
I tell my friends, they think I'm crazy,
What on earth will I do?

I am just too scared to look behind me,
Will it haunt me forever?
Will it ever stop following me?
I build up my courage and turn around to see that . . .
It was just my shadow!

Simon Islam (12)
Brecon High School

YELLOW

Daffodils trumpeting in the springtime
Buttercups dancing in the meadows,
Corn ripening in the fields,
Sunflowers growing straight and tall,
The golden sun glowing on the children playing.

Bethan Denley (12)
Brecon High School

MY DREAM

I'm standing on a big green carpet,
I hear the roaring of the crowd,
I look above, a sea of colour
Blasting songs and cheers aloud.

I hear the whistle, great excitement,
Rush across a ball in hand,
Put it down between the goalposts,
Win the game, joy across the land.

Proud I am to serve my country
And to help them win the game,
When I wake up from my dreamland,
I hope one day they'll know my name.

Ewan Williams (13)
Brecon High School

BLACK!

The creepy, night sky,
With the lucky cat,
the cauldron with a spell
and the superstitious witch,
the sad, stone walls,
they're coming to get you,
on a Hallowe'en night,
when the clock strikes
Midnight!

Jasmine Jones (11)
Brecon High School

FEAR POEM

When you have a fear or two,
Don't run and hide just like a shrew,
Express your fears and make them known,
They'll have gone when you have grown.

When you are scared, don't you hide,
Don't bottle your fears up inside,
Don't hide in a cupboard and never come out,
Call out your fear and shout, shout, shout.

Face your fears and look alive,
Come out of your house like a bee from a hive,
Bark like a dog and sting like a bee,
In the end you will be free.

Hannah Davies (12)
Brecon High School

THE COLOUR BLACK

An exploding bomb, blowing up buildings,
Coal from the mines, dirty-faced miners,
Frightened by spiders that hang from the ceiling.
Sizzling charcoal on the barbecue.
Black, billowing smoke from wet leaves on fire.
A black purring cat disturbs the night's peace.

Black!

Neil Patterson (11)
Brecon High School

IF ONLY

If only I could travel to New Zealand,
To see my auntie Sarah,
So I can talk to her,
So I can listen to her.

If only I could travel to New Zealand,
To see its geysers and boiling mud,
So I can watch them,
So I can see their power.

If only I could travel to New Zealand,
To see the ninety mile beach,
So I can see only sand,
So I can walk along it.

If only I could travel to New Zealand,
To see its wildlife,
So I can see kiwis,
So I can see tuis.

Ben Gibson (13)
Brecon High School

FEARS

My fear of family illness,
Which could come at any time,
Not moving paralysed,
Needing help.
Not breathing the country air,
Trapped inside the house,
With nothing to do, but wait.

My fear of family illness,
Not only a single person suffering,
But every member.
Nothing available to cure,
Helpless,
Scared of what could happen,
Will this illness
Come back to haunt us?

Eleri-Wyn Davies (12)
Brecon High School

END OF YEAR TESTS

Sunday night,
Nerves are up high,
Tests are coming,
I'm going to die!

Monday morning,
Tests are here,
Breathing deeply
And still in fear!

I sit,
Tests handed out,
Room in silence,
No one dare shout!

Scratching pens begin,
I sit and memorise,
I wish questions were easy,
I wish I had revised!

Rory Wolstenholme (12)
Brecon High School

MY DREAM

I was walking through a forest,
I was walking through a wood,
Somehow there were more trees,
Than there ever should.

I walked into a house,
I thought I saw a ghost
And I must admit,
It scared me the most.

I saw a bloody axe,
So I followed it to the shed
And the last place I rested,
Was in my death bed.

When I woke back up,
Breakfast was too soon,
When a big white ghost,
Came floating through my room!

Tomos Davies (12)
Brecon High School

WHITE

Pure as an angel's dress,
Rising froth from the sea,
Empty as an orphan's eye,
Polar bears scour the Antarctic,
Plain as soft snow,
Clouds sail the sky.

Sofie O'Shea (11)
Brecon High School

DREAM

A hot summer's day,
The sun is beaming,
Fish are jumping,
In the clear blue stream,
Birds are singing,
In the large oak tree,
Lambs are playing,
In the lush green field,
No more noise,
No more pollution,
No more greed.

Rhys Jones (12)
Brecon High School

A RABBIT'S LIFE

In a hutch all day,
All I want is to go out and play.

Lying down in the hot sun,
All I want is to have some fun.

I want to go out and see my mates,
But instead I'm stuck behind gates.

Trying to run and stretch my legs,
But all I can do is beg and beg.

Wanting to go out and roam,
Wish someone would take me to a good home.

If I was allowed out to play,
I am happy, I would say.

Rebecca Williams (13)
King Henry VIII School

THE HILLS AND THE MOUNTAINS

Today I see the world is different,
We have twisted it, like a torrent.

But still, the hills remain unhurt,
They have not been covered with dirt.

They are grassy, fresh and great,
They remain unspoilt through ages of late.

The valley's have been plundered,
The seashores, they lay blundered.

The strong hills stand bold beside the mountains,
As you venture, you see the old fountains.

These are the remnants from the past,
That will lay there until the last.

The mountains grew in the early days,
While the others went in different ways.

Today I see the world is different,
We have twisted it, like a torrent.

Craig Matthews (13)
King Henry VIII School

THE CREATURE

I am lying on this bed,
What should I do?
I look down at my body,
Of everything is two,
Two legs, two arms,
Two hands and feet!
Why has everyone left me?
There is no one to greet.

I am very lonely, very frightened,
Extremely sad am I.
Who am I? Where did I come from?
Oh so many questions, I just want to cry.
Look! My arms are moving,
My legs too, I am walking across the room,
I hope someone finds me,
I want my questions to be answered soon.

Samantha Rice (12)
King Henry VIII School

LOOKING BACK AT INDIA

I must go back to India,
For there're so many things to do,
Whilst being there,
I wanted to disappear,
For everyone was Hindu.
I gradually grew fond of people smiling
And staring at me,
For a white person there,
Is very rare to see.
Then there are Varanasi,
Which I found the worst,
All the pollution, all of the traffic,
I simply wanted to burst.

My favourite place was Goa,
It simply had to be,
With the beach outside my doorstep,
The white sand and clear blue sea.

Charlie Lewis (13)
King Henry VIII School

BROTHERS AND SISTERS

My brother hates me and I hate him
And that's what makes him special,
I could love him,
But he wouldn't love me,
So why do I bother?
Because he's my brother,
Although we fight and tears are shed,
We always make up just before bed,
My brother hates me and I hate him
And that's what makes him special.

My sister loves me and I love her
And that's what I like best
Although we get angry
And punches are thrown,
She's always the one,
That doesn't leave me alone,
If I am picked on,
She gives them a kick on
And always saves the day,
But if they are younger
Or have a big brother,
She runs the other way.

Morgan Smith (13)
King Henry VIII School

HENRY

I have a dog called Henry,
He is a basset but sometimes a asset
His ears are long and often pong,
He runs fast through the wood,
Like a basset should.

He sits on the mat by the cat,
He is lemon and white but never bites,
He eats like a pig but he doesn't wear a wig,
I always give him a cooch,
Cause he's my little pooch.

Helen Crowle (14)
King Henry VIII School

WORLD

The world is round like a sphere,
In Russia, it's very cold here,
Antarctica is full of ice,
Spain is hot and very nice.

Waves, caves all around the world,
Planes, trains everywhere,
Sunny, hot in Africa,
Cold, freezing in Antarctica.

Poor and hungry in South Africa,
Rich and selfish in America,
That's what these countries are like,
It's difficult to live in these conditions.

Hot in the Sahara for many days,
Rain in Thailand, it's like this always,
Windy in Wales,
Rainy in England.

Cold, hot weather,
Poor and rich places,
Windy and rainy conditions,
That's the world!

Sam Morgan (11)
King Henry VIII School

THE WORLD

This is a poem about the world,
All the pain and hurt around us,
How lives are lost,
For no reason or for our queen and country?

The world is not such a happy place,
All the wars and deaths within the world,
Take September 11th, all those lives wasted,
Or World War I & II but brave were the soldiers doomed to die.

Sarah, Milly, Jessica and Holly and other children killed,
What had they done wrong? Why did they have to be taken away?
Long black nights and days waiting for the phone call
'I am OK, I'm safe.'
Innocent children lured into a black hole.

Why do we have to be at war?
I'll tell you war is the wrong answer!
Abduction, death, war, starvation! The only question is why?
Children living in hope that one day soon
They will eat more than beans or bread!

All the world's people can do is hope and pray,
That it will all stop!
Could we become a loving world
Instead of war, abduction and everything else?
Would we be willing to love each and every person around us?
Though most are bad!

Maybe some day it will all end!
'Heal the world
Make it a
Better place!'

Lydia Price (11)
King Henry VIII School

FEELINGS

I feel scared,
Unhappy, lonely,
Sad, upset and angry.

I feel joyful,
Happy and light,
Skippy, bouncy and jolly.

I feel miserable,
Frightened and terrible,
Screaming, crying, alone.

I feel cheerful,
Glad, gleeful,
Merry joyous and delightful.

I feel blue,
Dismal, gloomy,
Grave, moody and sober.

I feel thrilled,
Festive, gay,
Proud, radiant and lively.

I feel grim,
Glum and mournful,
Guilty, sorry and remorseful.

I feel excellent,
Excited, blissful,
Pleased, blessed and fortunate.

I feel hopeless,
Troubled by life,
Ghoulish, depressed and . . . dead.

Holly O'Farrell (11)
King Henry VIII School

Dark And Cold Night

As the night drew in,
It was getting cold,
Standing in a field.

I was on my own,
Starting to moan,
Waiting for someone to come and go.

The breeze got colder,
I felt as if I was getting older,
But it was a long, long night.

I heard foxes howling,
I was sitting down crying,
Still waiting for someone to shout hello.

As I walked through the trees,
I felt a heavier breeze,
Fell to the ground and begged please.

A shadow came towards me,
I didn't know if it was coming to save me,
He opened his arms and I knew I was safe.

He picked me up,
It was pure luck,
He took me home and I realised I wasn't alone.

Anna Forsyth (15)
King Henry VIII School

My Bike

My bike is good,
My bike is sweet,
I ride my bike,
Every other week.

It's better than football
And running around a pitch,
My bike is faster,
Than Ryan Giggs.

Lee Hatherall (13)
King Henry VIII School

UNTITLED

Football this, football that,
This is the gossip of the week.

Free kicks, goal kicks, everything is a kick,
There are 11 players on the pitch, on the pitch, on the pitch.

Footie, oi,
Footie, footie, oi, oi,
Footie, footie, footie, oi, oi, oi.

The rules have changed every year,
Every year, every year.

I play for a team
We play hard every match,
Just to try to win.

When our opponents score a goal,
Our trainer tells us to keep our heads up,
So we should score a goal or two.

Football!

Geraint Howells (12)
King Henry VIII School

FOOTBALL

I like football
The way it is,
A loud cheering,
Game, it's easy,
To score a goal
Or two and
It's easy to run
And pass the
Ball back and forth.
If you were a football
Player what would
You do, would you sit
Around and be lazy
Or come and play too.

People are shooting all at once,
The goalkeeper is in a big rush,
You play a match,
You score a goal,
Now is the time to say goodbye!

Kurt Kelly (12)
King Henry VIII School

I LOVE!

I love quite a lot of things,
Like family and friends,
Like brothers and sisters,
OK, maybe not!

I love quite a lot of things,
Like hockey and netball,
Like football and rounders,
Yes, I like them all!

I love quite a lot of things,
Like chocolate teddy bears,
Like my mum's cream cakes!
Mmmmm! I love them all!

I love quite a lot of things,
Like the swift of my mum's perfume,
Like the smell of the fresh air
As I walk out the door!

Chelsea Viveash (12)
King Henry VIII School

FRIENDS

Friendship is a very
Important thing, without
Friends you are a loner,
You get teased and called names,
Don't put yourself in that position.

Don't treat your friends like dirt,
Treat them the way you would like
To be treated, otherwise you will have
No friends, so show respect to
Gain respect and care.

I have good friends who do respect and care,
I've had them all my life and they would
Look after me as I would look after them.
We have our ups and downs
But we are basically like sisters.

I know how it feels to have friends
Who are fake, so check, they could
Just be using you.

Jessica Jones (11)
King Henry VIII School

LIFE IN THE HOOD

I walk through the back streets of LA
Apparently it's like this every day
All I can see is blood, guts and guns,
This certainly isn't the place for nuns,
Gang wars in the street, every day,
People getting shot every which way,
Gangsters walking past,
How long's this going to last?

You stand there in the street,
The whole gang staring at you,
A whole bunch of thugs,
Pumped up with drugs,
Which way are you going to run?
Take out your gun,
Before somebody takes out theirs
And without a care,
Releases a bullet into the air.

You're not coming out of the gang,
You're in there for good,
You better stay loyal and not turn your back,
On the people who trust you,
Took you into their gang,
What are you going to do?

On the run from the cops, 24/7,
When you die, you aren't going to Heaven,
Drugs and guns aren't doing you any good,
Are you sure you like this life in the hood?
One wrong move and you're out of the gang,
Your life is over with the sound of a bang,
You'll lay on the floor, the gang laughing at you,
You don't like the life on the run now, do you?

Tom Carrett (13)
King Henry VIII School

WHAT'S GOING ON?

What is going on in the world today?
Poverty, and war every day.
If the minority cares, nothing is going to change,
But help is just too little, it's not too late.
Around the world there is too much hate.
People destroy, and choose not to create.

Thousands of people spread across nations,
Die in pain of severe starvation.
A look at their food supply is enough of a demonstration,
Of what they live and die through, of their great patience.
A hassle in our lives now seems to be just a small complication.
In comparison our standard houses are palaces like accommodation.

Children are often taught that violence is so wrong,
But frequently it's the news which has just gone.
No co-operation means the violence is prolonged.
Even more deaths, the list getting long.
Days of killing and bloodshed go on and on,
Deaths on both sides, only evil has won.

Shadi Abdel-Gadir (13)
King Henry VIII School

FOOTBALL ON A SUNDAY

I wake up on the break of day,
I get up to have my breakfast,
Then I get dressed into my football kit,
We get into the car and drive wherever we are playing,
I get on the pitch and think -
Are we going to win?

Ben Howland (11)
King Henry VIII School

THE ENVIRONMENT

T   he world is round and blue and bluey-green,
H   owever on the surface it isn't all it seems,
E   verywhere you go there are problems on the scene.

E   very government on earth is trying to get rid of litter,
N   ever has this problem been so bad,
V   ery much a bigger problem we have at the moment,
I   t's called *Global Warming*,
R   estless gases escape in our car fumes, bouncing back to Earth,
O   h they heat up the atmosphere, they melt the polar ice caps
causing rising waters.
N   ow to another issue, the energy crisis.
M   ore and more fossil fuels are being used. They aren't
endless sources.
E   very power source will run out except for one . . .
N   uclear power. This is the most dangerous power source,
it heats up particles to make a dangerous almost endless
power source.
T   here, you know now the problems of the world.
Next time, you have litter, don't throw it, put it in the bin
And don't leave your light on all night, turn it off!

Treat the world kindly!

Adam Connell (11)
King Henry VIII School

THE GLISTENING BALL OF FIRE

I sit here alone and sparkling,
Glistening in the day,
Shining down on Earth
And sending down my rays.

At night I get to sleep,
Though only for a while,
Then rise up in the morning,
Bright eyed and bushy tailed.

Christie Ellen Russell (13)
King Henry VIII School

THE THUNDERSTORM

Yellow flashing of light racing through the sky,
Rumbling noise of thunder in the far distance,
Yellow bolts of lightning flying towards earth
Then the rain comes.

Sounds of thunder screeching through the street,
As people race to get out of the rain,
Grey clouds coming together to block out the sun
The thunderstorm is worse.

Gallons of water pouring out of the clouds,
Bolts of lightning brighten the sky,
Explosions of thunder skate the earth
People start to tremble.

The clouds start to separate but it still rains,
The thunder becomes quieter but can still be heard,
The lightning becomes dimmer but can still be seen
People seem to be calming.

The clouds disappear and so does the rain,
The thunder is silent and it becomes peaceful,
The lightning has stopped and nothing can be seen,
People have calmed.

Jamie Smith (12)
King Henry VIII School

HAPPINESS IS ...

Happiness is having toys and games,
Happiness is having lots of fame,
Or is it?
Happiness means to be joyful and gay,
Happiness is having the time to play,
Happiness is having amusements galore,
Happiness is to never be bored,
Is it really?
Happiness is having nice clothes and a house,
Happiness is having a cute pet mouse,
Happiness is to have a nice tea,
Happiness means to have fun and be free!
But what is happiness really?
Happiness is to have friends up above,
Happiness is having a family and love,
That's what happiness is to me!

Natasha Matthews (14)
King Henry VIII School

MOUNTAINS

We're so lucky living among seven mountains,
Seven beautiful views of our Welsh valley,
Seven places to be nearer our God,
Seven outdoor cathedrals,
Seven birds eye view's of farmland, canals and rivers,
Seven has always been considered a lucky number,
Seven reminds me of home and how lucky I am to live in
Abergavenny.

Lewis Froggatt (11)
King Henry VIII School

CHRISTMAS TIME

The tree is 6 foot tall,
The lights are shiny bright,
The snow starts to fall,
Snowmen there and everywhere,
Christmas spirit is here,
In shops, on TV, on billboards,
On the 24th,
Kids get excited,
They jump around and run around,
At half-past nine,
They are sent to bed,
They put milk, carrots and cookies out,
They are to go straight to sleep,
On the 25th they wake up,
Everyone to go downstairs,
A bike, a toy, a game there and here,
This is Christmas time.

Lewis Smith (13)
King Henry VIII School

ME AND MY JOB

Hi I've got the best job
In the world . . . (working in a chippy).
I get absolutely loads of money,
(£10.00 a month) I am a loaded man.
I've got a lush sports car,
(Yeah right, I've got a banger worth
About £100 or £200).
Anyway got to go to work in
My chippie chippie chippie.

Jack George (11)
King Henry VIII School

DOGS AREN'T JUST FOR CHRISTMAS

On a Christmas Day
I was taken away,
To a house far past my sight.
The girls and boys
Made so much noise,
I was in total fright.

When the kids were away,
On one stormy day,
I was glared at by the man,
Quite madly,
The man grabbed me
And stuffed me into a van.

I was hauled by my knees,
Thrown into the trees,
I thought it was a game at first,
Off the man went,
To the wild I was sent,
Tears in my eyes did burst,
Dogs aren't just for Christmas.

Stephen J Monaghan (13)
King Henry VIII School

LOVE

Love is a flower,
Love is a bee,
Love is a power,
That you cannot see.

It's trapped in your heart
And hurts when let out,
Love is easy to start,
When you know what it's about.

Love is a desire,
Full of sorrow and pain,
Happiness is just an admirer,
But deep in your heart, dreams remain.

After love has gone,
You'll never forget,
The cheerful song,
You had once met.

Gemma Whitehead (13)
King Henry VIII School

RUNNING

This is it!
The night before the big marathon,
Physically prepare,
Mentally prepare,
Eat some fruit and vegetables,
Get my kit sorted out,
For
Tomorrow.
It is late in the night
And I'm going to bed,
In the morning I have to get up,
I put on my kit and walk out of the door,
Everyone was there,
At the big race!
We all started to run,
The sound was like a stampede,
The finish line was a few yards away,
So I started to sprint,
Yes!
I won.

Christopher Foulkes (11)
King Henry VIII School

TREACLE PIE

I once had a chestnut pony,
Her name was Treacle Pie,
Whenever I tried to ride her,
She threw me to the sky!

One day my pony and I,
Were plodding down the road,
Suddenly I heard a squish,
She had trodden on a toad!

She walked away as cool as ice,
So I looked at her and said,
'Oh you naughty pony Treacle!
You're going home and straight to bed!'

Another day, poor Treacle fell ill
And for once, I had nothing to say,
The vet came and said that Treacle,
Would be fine in one or two days.

One or two days came and went,
I began to get very afraid,
I decided to give Treacle some Calpol
But it turned her dapple-grey!

Megan Bransom (14)
King Henry VIII School

MY LIFE

My alarm goes off,
I turn it off,
My life.

I get out of bed,
Go in the bathroom,
My life.

Have my breakfast,
Get ready,
My life.

Get to school,
Start my lesson,
My life.

Jodie Hughes (11)
King Henry VIII School

THE SEA IN ALL ITS GLORY

T imid clouds from across the sky,
H ulls float through a blanket of water,
E ndless rows of rocks.

S ky of blue turning grey,
E merald sea shows a warning,
A ll around, the wind blows harder.

I ncreasing waves crash,
N ever-ending.

A ll around the wind blows stronger,
L ightning flashes, thunder rumbles,
L ighting up the sky so bright.

I t seems to last forever, but then,
T urning skies back to blue
S unshine shines brightly.

G littering shadows form,
L ittle waves appear,
O rdinary life begins, once again.
R esting,
Y et silent.

Laura Price (11)
King Henry VIII School

HEAVEN AND HELL

Heaven seems a delightful place,
Fairies, leprechauns and gods amazing grace,
Angels and cherubs serving and treating your every need
And banning your past sins like jealousy and greed.
Apparently in Heaven, you can do whatever you please,
No bills, loans or doctors fees.
In my Heaven there would be chocolate and sweets,
Family and friends and other types of treats.

Hell seems a dreadful place,
Flames of fire and a devilish face,
Hell reminds people of pitchforks and knives,
But for all you know, it could be full of coachroaches and beehives,
Trembling shadows and screams in your ear,
Threats and abuse bellowed at you that no one else can hear,
Waiting around in your chamber dark,
For your lunch of snails, dogs tongues and a live great white shark,
I'd prefer to go to Heaven than Hell,
Without Saturn ringing his big old bell.

Nesta Watkins (12)
King Henry VIII School

WAR, PLAY TIME

War, play time,
What's the difference?
One's happy,
One's sad.

Bombs fly everywhere,
Kids shout and scream,
Evacuate I hear,
Laughter I hear.

War, play time,
What's the difference?
Dead people,
Alive people,
That's the difference.

Stephanie Macpherson (14)
King Henry VIII School

MY FAMILY

First of all there is me,
Quite brilliant as you can see,
I always try my very best,
Now lets see about the rest.

Well my sister,
Is an expert at Twister,
Sometimes we fight,
But I think she's alright.

What can I say about my brother?
He's like no other,
He can be really vain
And a right pain.

Now about my dad,
When I see him it makes me glad,
He is quite tall
And spoils us all.

Mum would then be last in line,
She is usually feeling fine,
She is there for us all,
Almost always on call.

Helena Nilsson (12)
King Henry VIII School

Too Late!

You know he's the one for you,
He's Mr Right, it's so true,
You like him, he likes you,
It's time you thought it through.

Get that guy before it's too late,
You think you know what love is, you're in a state,
Charm him now before he's taken,
If you don't it's your heart that'll be aching.

He rings your bell, he gets you going,
It's your true feelings you need to be showing,
It's your time now, time to shine,
Having feelings for someone isn't a crime.

Get that guy before it's too late,
You think you know what love is, you're in a state,
Be yourself, don't start faking,
If you don't it's your heart that'll be aching.

You see him often he's mostly around,
But when you see him you don't make a sound,
He fits your description of the perfect guy,
You need to learn not to be shy.

Get that guy before it's too late,
You think you know what love is, you're in a state,
The perfect couple that's what you'd be making,
If you don't it's your heart that'll be aching!

Chloe Williams (12)
King Henry VIII School

STREET PREDATOR

Cars like cheetahs sprinting past you,
Their teeth glow bright, a menacing glare,
The eyes are so wide, you can see in,
The owners going crazy behind the wheel,
The beastly bodywork giving a gleam of proudness,
Prowling the streets looking for food,
This fierce animal has found a victim,
Guzzling the blood it is now recharged,
Off home this savage is to go,
Back to his lair, to hide there,
Away from the rain, to rest until he needs to feast again,
As his glare does drown,
His eyes do darken, he's off to sleep for his strength to harden.

Adele Morgan (12)
King Henry VIII School

MISS MILLIE

Her eyes glisten like stars in the darkness.
Her nose is like a shiny pink button.
Her teeth are as sharp as needles.
Her tail is like a flag waving in the breeze.
Her fur coat is as smooth as silk and shimmers in the sun.
She elegantly walks like she is the boss with her long sleek body.
She secretly spies as quiet as a mouse for her prey.
She eats like there's no tomorrow.
She leaps like a frog with her long thin legs.
She hisses and spits like a snake.
At the end of the day she falls into an endless sleep.

Carolyn McAughey (13)
King Henry VIII School

PLACES!

If you want to go on holiday
You might get carried away
So many places to choose from
The people make up a song
Then you don't want to be too long

       If you want to choose a sunny place
       So then you get a tanned face
       Choose Florida, Brazil or Mexico
       And then you lay down low
       So then the stars can glow

Or you want a cool holiday
From a place not far away
Choose France, Sweden or the Alps
So then you don't get a burnt scalp

       But you might want to put those together
       So then it might be better
       Choose France that's the best place to go
       Then you will enjoy the flow
       But now you can't choose so

So now the best holiday would be
To stay with your family to see
No exotic place not far away
You want to stay
So now you don't want to go away.

Mitchell Lawrence (11)
King Henry VIII School

TWO POSH LADIES

From my window I can see,
Two posh ladies with a cup of tea.
Sitting outside in the rain,
On the corner of my lane.
One says, 'Ooo', the other says, 'Oh,'
From the sky came a ball of snow.
It hits them both on the head,
My sister heard, got out of bed.
Down the stairs one, two, three,
Out the door, my sister and me.
We heard the ladies wail and groan,
My sister got her mobile phone.
She dialled quickly nine, nine, nine,
The ambulance man said they'd be fine.
He said, 'We'll be just one minute,
We're taking pictures of Mr Linnet.'
When the ambulance did come,
One of the men started to hum.
He said they would be better soon
And would not come to a snowy doom.
All they needed was a rest,
To bring them up to their best.
So we went back to bed and sleep
And no one ever heard a peep
From those two ladies in their beds,
Who had big lumps on both their heads.

Jemima Labisch (13)
King Henry VIII School

A DOLPHIN'S VIEW

Every morning I wake up to catch the sunrise,
But instead all I see is a huge crowd of people.
I turn round and I am in a small swimming pool,
Not the ocean,
Four walls and no fish to eat,
The only way to get food is to be an act of entertainment.

Once I have finished my act,
I go behind a screen to an even smaller pool,
Not enough for me to lie in or even swim,
There are four of us trying to fit in a three by three metre pool.
On the walls are painted plants and sea creatures
To replace the real thing.

If I jump high enough I can see the ocean
And on some days I can see my family,
Who at night call me to go home to them.
The only thing is . . . I can't!

Jessica Scarisbrick (13)
King Henry VIII School

OH HOW WOULD IT BE!

Oh how would it be,
To be a fish in the sea,
To swim around all day,
Especially in May.

Jellyfish gliding past,
Watch out for a shark,
It moves very fast,
Slimy seaweed swaying to and fro,
Looking for my friend called Mo.

Exploring the ocean bed,
Looking at coral that is red,
Oh how would it be,
To be a fish in the sea.

Caryl Auty (12)
King Henry VIII School

THE GREAT BIG BLISTER

I have a sister,
With a great big blister,
It's about a metre long,
About as tall as my cousin John.
She tries real hard to get it to pop,
But if she can't she blows her top.
But one really successful day,
In a barn on top of some hay,
My sister found a bright shiny pin,
About as long as a fish's fin.
She pulled off her shoe and her sock,
Gave it a prick and then it went pop!
She started to cry,
Because it stung her eye,
I said to calm down,
To her face with a frown.
She started to nag about how much it hurt,
And she started to spit on my best T-shirt!
But, now my friend,
It has come to an end,
About my sister,
Who had a great big blister!

Hollie Jones (11)
King Henry VIII School

TRAVELLING

Travelling slow,
Travelling fast,
No time to stop
As we have got to go somewhere hot,
Travelling slow,
Travelling fast,
The journey has just began, the time does not pass.

Travelling slow,
Travelling fast,
No time to stop
As we have got to go somewhere romantic,
Travelling slow,
Travelling fast,
The journey is in the middle so we are nearly there at last.

Travelling slow,
Travelling fast,
There is nowhere to go so we have to go home at last,
Travelling slow,
Travelling fast,
The journey is at the end at last.

Nowhere to go,
Just home sweet home,
Time for more travelling,
Next time we pass.

Claire Pugh (13)
King Henry VIII School

THE SNOWFLAKE

I see its sparkle
Glittering in the light
As it's falling
Gliding like a kite.

It joins its friends,
Upon the ground,
Where it gracefully lands
Without a sound.

The flakes link up
And form a cover,
Producing a sight,
Like no other.

Pure and white,
The carpet glows,
I really love it,
When it snows.

Georgina Jones (11)
King Henry VIII School

EXPERIENCE EXCITEMENT

Start your engines!
Pick up speed,
Look out for flags,
Stop in the pit,
Rip around sharp corners,
Brake suddenly
Smash bollards out of place.

Daniel Corran (13)
King Henry VIII School

WATER

Water, fresh as it falls over stones down the stream.
The gentle silk screen of water as it springs
From the purple headed mountain.
Sheep drink the pure, ice-cold water to satisfy their thirst.
It's like Heaven.
Fish who are as silver as steel swim upstream enjoying its pure taste.
Children swim in the river that is as clear as crystal.
They try to fight the current.
Birds of all colours sweep down to get the creepy insects
Off the water's surface.
Otters swim swiftly under the blue water.
They dart through the weeds with a playful nature.

James David Lane (12)
King Henry VIII School

THE BIG BANG

Nothing but blackness was all around,
Until the big bang went *boom!*
Right out loud!

This was the moment the world began,
The first step towards the creation of man,

The mountains and seas,
The plants and the trees,
The reptiles and mammals,
The people and animals.

A miracle happened then and there,
The world taught us all to love and to care!

Kelly Jones (11)
King Henry VIII School

THE MATCH

We went to the match today
To watch Leeds United play
When the players came on
The crowd sang a song
We came to watch the Villa
It's going to be a thriller
The referee blew for play
The crowd shouted *hooray!*
When Bowyer got the ball
We thought he was going to score
The crowd began to roar
They thought the Villa would score
It ended as a bore
As a nil-nil draw.

Victoria Katherine Rigby (11)
King Henry VIII School

MY FAMILY!

I have a mum and dad,
Two sisters that drive me mad.
One older, one younger,
Both as bad as one another.
The dogs are always barking,
Yap yap yap!
Until they have their dinner,
Then they'll have a *nap!*
My gran is sitting in her chair,
Reading her Woman's Weekly,
But also needles in her cardi,
For sewing is her hobby!

Rachael Cochrane (11)
King Henry VIII School

MY DOG

I have a dog who's very good
He is white and black and likes a good pat.
We go for walks down the park
Where he runs around and likes to bark.
He runs to meet me at the gate
But oh what a lot of fuss he makes
He leaps and jumps all around and rolls
And tumbles on the ground.
When we tell him to sit or beg
Then tell him to go to bed.
He stops and listens to what we say.
He is a looney in every way
But I must tell you his name is Sparky
And he is a great spark in every way.
He is my friend I will always treasure
Because he gives us so much pleasure.
We go for walks, I only wish he could talk
So we could tell each other secrets.
As we all know we have no regrets
Sparky is one of the best.
My dog.

Ayrton Pugh (11)
King Henry VIII School

MONDAY AGAIN

Monday again
And there they go,
Off to work,
Leaving me alone.

I'm left in a cage,
With a bowl of food,
Something to drink,
Leaving me to brood.

No one to talk to,
No one to play with,
All I do
Is sleep all day.

My life is boring,
My life is so bad,
I wish I was somewhere else
Because I'm going mad!

Aled Rees (13)
King Henry VIII School

A WALK IN THE PARK

Today I went to the park
All the dogs around started to bark.

Sarah and I played with the ball
And then I heard someone call.

It was her friend Liz with Jack
Jack started to attack but I got him back.

We ran off and found a river
I had a swim but I started to shiver.

I hate a wet coat, oh my!
Now it'll take ages to dry.

I went up to a tree
And did a humungous wee!

It's a dog's life!

Sophie Bensley (11)
King Henry VIII School

THE BEST PLACE FOR ME WOULD BE . . .

The best place for me would be
In Pembrokeshire right by the sea,
From our caravan upon the hill,
You can look across the sea so still.

On the bright and sunny days,
You can walk around the bays.
Up the hills and down the cliffs,
Find a rock and have a whiff!

On a boring, windy day,
You can go outside and play
If there is a storm that's blowing
You can sit inside and do some sewing.

Then when I'm tucked up in my bed
I hear those seagulls overhead
I think about the day that's past
It really has been quite a blast

I can't imagine, I wish you could see
Our quiet caravan by the sea
It really just has to be
The very best place for me.

Chloe Havard (11)
King Henry VIII School

HORSES IN WINTER

The horses in their stables
Keeping nice and warm
While staring out at the winter down
Some are eating crunchy oats
Others growing their thick winter coats

Some horses wearing rugs
Keeping all warm and snug
And they run around in the snow
Just look how fast they go!
Covered with the soft white snow.

Nicola Davies (11)
King Henry VIII School

LUKE'S POEM

My holiday this year was to Cornwall,
What a wonderful place it is to play,
Some days we played beach football
And some days we went surfing all day.

The beaches were long and sandy,
The sea was warm and blue,
The shop on the beach sold candy,
Specially for me and you.

In the town were shops that sold pasties,
Said to be the best in the west,
My mum says they are nasties,
After putting one to the test.

My brother wanted to go on a boat trip,
That ran all around the bay,
But Mum said a trip on a ship,
Was not for her today.

I always hook a crab when I go fishing,
And if I don't I reel a fish,
Only one because I am wishing
When I land one I'll put it on the dish.

Luke Tagg (11)
King Henry VIII School

THE WORLD

The sea is blue
The land is green
Sometimes I'm kind
Sometimes I'm mean

The clouds are white
The sky is black at night
The sun is hot and sunny
And when it's warm
Everyone feels funny.

People are tall
Some are small
Babies are tiny and sweet
They have little tiny hands and feet.

Carl Cantle (11)
King Henry VIII School

FREE

Flying high through the sky,
The wind beneath my wings.
Flying as high as a bird
Free to go wherever my heart may take me.
My limits?

My own imagination.

Zoe Passariello (13)
King Henry VIII School

SOCCER, CRICKET

I love football,
Football loves me,
Playing for Chelsea
Is my dream.

My summer sport is cricket,
To take lots of wickets
And to score plenty of runs
Is my dream.

For both sports
You should play as a team,
To play for a top club
Is my dream.

Robert Bradley (11)
King Henry VIII School

DOGS

Spots and patches
Long and short hair
Big blue eyes
Glaring everywhere

Long and short tails
Sharp claws
Wagging tails
Padded paws

All shapes and sizes
Big and small
Furry and fluffy
I love them all!

Lucy Watkins (13)
King Henry VIII School

THE BLUEBIRD

There sat a bluebird
high up in the tree
singing his tuneful song
right back down at me.

He stopped for a while
and what I could see
was the bird leave his perch
and fly right past me.

Still singing in flight
his feathers aflutter
he became quiet
not even a mutter.

Maybe he was tired
or just glad to be
off his perch
and out of that tree.

Samantha John (12)
King Henry VIII School

SPACE

S   pace is a dark, mysterious world.
P   lanets that are unknown lurk in the dismal darkness,
A   stronauts explore this obscure place hoping to find
    something amazing.
C   enturies pass, space is still holding its secret,
E   veryone puzzled by this unsolved mystery!

Mercedes McMaster (11)
King Henry VIII School

PETS

Pets are our best friends,
They're always pleased to see you;
You'd think I'd been away for a month
If I'm five minutes late.

Pets if you play and feed them well,
They'll love you without question,
All they ask for is your love
And some attention.

Pets they come in all shapes and sizes,
Dogs, cats and rabbits
They love you without question,
Then why are some people so cruel?

Ieuan Davies (11)
King Henry VIII School

MY SISTER

I look at my sister
I don't see an angel
I see a devil
Who calls me names

Instead of a halo
All I see are horns
Instead of a white gown
All I see is red skin

I knew this wasn't my sister
I heard a ring and woke up
I saw my real sister
It was all a dream.

Gary Barrett (12)
King Henry VIII School

THE MOUNTAINS OF CHILDHOOD

The lonely mountains on the moor
Cried and screeched till they could do it no more.
Then came the purple pink flowers spreading,
Moving across the rocky cliff
I skipped and ran through the sweet smelling trees.
I had a peep at nests and caves of things beyond my age.
It was so quiet a silence which went on forever.
It was clever and knew all the best spots of horses leaping,
Lambs creeping and birds swooping high, high up.
The sound here was alive, the breeze moving through my silky hair.
I'd climb trees and eat apples, kiwis and pears.
I love the mountain where you could run and run
And never stop until your legs went pop.
The city here is dull and loud of beeping cars and rustling crowds.
I dream about going back to those mountains,
The mountains of joy freedom and excitement.

Lucy O'Byrne (11)
King Henry VIII School

THE ANIMAL OF MIGHTY STRENGTH

The dragon with eyes of flame
The bull with muscles of steel
The crocodile with jaws of mighty strength
The cheetah with his frightful speed
The grizzly bear with a fearsome swoop
The snake with his powerful strike
Put them all together you would
Have an unbeatable animal.

Thomas Davies (12)
King Henry VIII School

JUMPING LESSONS

You've just tacked up and you're ready to go,
You're ready to go cantering round the school,
The wind blowing through your hair,
The thunder of the horse's hooves as they hit dusty ground.

You're going to jump,
You turn the corner of the school,
You know you must go in a dead straight line,
You're just seconds away
Jumping position,
Wee . . . *bump!*
You made it,
Now time to get off,
Pay, go home!

Charmaine Cunningham (11)
King Henry VIII School

MY FAMILY

I love my mum with all my heart
She's really kind and nice and smart.
I love my dad, my stepmum too,
There's Jasmine Holmes and lots to do.
I love my nan, she's very nice,
In her food there's lots of spice.
My grandpa Jack likes every rabbit,
Looking after them has become a habit.
I love my nanny, her name is Viv,
She's good at cooking with a sieve.
My granda Robin's a computer whizz
The things he does, put my nanny in a tizz!

Jason Holmes (11)
King Henry VIII School

WHY ME

Why did it have to be? Why?
I didn't pick to be the leader
People, you stupid people
Why do you follow me?
Why? Why? Why?
You should do what you want
Don't copy me in what I do
Be yourself, you lifeless people
How can I forget that all you do is . . .
How can I be an individual?
You are all leaches on me
And I am the thing
You suck on my personality
On who I am, me not you
Be yourself, why do you have to be me
Why not a popular kid, no it has to be . . .
Me the one who likes this
But no one else does
Me the one who likes a
Certain thing which you don't
Why? Why? Why?
I don't like all these people, know one different
All the same all one person
Just me, but no I'm wrong everyone's me.

Adelle Faulds (12)
King Henry VIII School

MY POSTMAN

My postman is a fellow with a big loud bellow.
My grandma called him Billy but my neighbour said that's silly.
But Mum likes him most when he delivers post.

Holly Menzies (11)
King Henry VIII School

AUTUMN'S HERE

The air is going misty
And the leaves are going crispy.
The trees are going bald
And the weather is going cold.

The squirrels are crawling,
Where the nuts are falling.
The nights are getting longer
And the winds are getting stronger.

But I will be warm and snug,
Like a bug in a rug.
When I've got my central heating
On full blast!

Thomas West (11)
King Henry VIII School

MY SKATEBOARD AND I

My skateboard is like my shadow,
We travel everywhere together.
We nose slide on the grind rail,
Over the death box we sail.
Kick flip over the fun box,
Pop shove it into the foam pit.
It's thrilling dropping the vert ramp
And dark sliding over the spine.
Roll into a quarter-pipe
And do a rock and roll!
My skateboard and I.

Calum Vaughan (12)
King Henry VIII School

HERE COMES AUTUMN

Here comes autumn speeding up the road,
Here I am, I haven't been told!
You can, by the leaves,
That summer is gone, so is greenery too.

Here comes autumn, soon to be here!
The goodbye to summer, that is what I fear . . . and
That the cold weather, will start soon
I hope it will not come this afternoon.

Go away autumn, you are too cold,
Not to keep warm . . . you need to be bold
Why are you coming, do you hate summer so?
Would it be something else if you said no?

Summer, oh summer where could you be?
I cannot handle this weather . . . too cold for me!
I think it won't stop, well not for me.
Mother Nature please hear my plea!

Mark Butler (11)
King Henry VIII School

FOOTBALL

I like to play football
I find it fun
Sometimes I get angry
And lash out
I try my best sometimes
That is the problem.

My friends help me control my temper
I play for Cardiff City
The people there are funny
Mel and Della
They even gave me a jacket
To wear anywhere.

Craig Norman (11)
King Henry VIII School

PEMBROKE CASTLE

Pembroke Castle is near the sea
Its towering walls are made of stone.
The castle stands upon a hill
From everywhere that's what you see.

The defensive towers stand tall
And can be seen from far away.
The great stone keep has spiral
Steps that wind around outside the wall.

Inside the walls is a huge green lawn
With remains of buildings that are no more
The tower overlooking the river
Is where King Henry VII was born.

When you're outside on the grass
The sun is warm on your head.
When you're inside the tower
You're cold in the crumbled mass.

Tom Jayne (11)
King Henry VIII School

ALL ABOUT ME

My name is Sam and I'm eleven
Just started KHS and I'm in year seven.
I'm into rugby, fishing and lots more.
Skateboarding's the main hobby I adore.
To grind down my pole, or jump off my ramp,
When I pull off an ollie I feel like a champ.
Fishing's alright, I go with my dad
Didn't catch a thing last week, how sad.
Rugby's a laugh, I made the team,
Keep up the training, must show to be keen.
I'm a blue belt in tae kwon do.
The koren is tough,
I like the sparing part but we don't do enough.
Going on my motorbike cheers up my day
Revving over jumps up and away.
Well that's all I can tell you right now you see,
As my friends are waiting outside for me.

Sam Richards (11)
King Henry VIII School

COURT

A man was sent to court for a crime,
They didn't even argue, not a single bit.
Only because the man's brother was the judge.
He walked out of the court gates
Without a single feeling of guilt showing on his face.

Luke Harris (11)
King Henry VIII School

THE TOWN

Cars hurtled through the busy streets,
Policemen marched on their beats,
Shoppers hurried into shops,
Children sucking lollipops,
Teenagers doing drugs, smoking,
Taxi drivers waiting, joking,
Shops start closing,
Tramps start dozing,
Landlords start to open their pubs,
A while to wait until the late-night clubs,
Youths loitering in the dark alleyways,
Toy shop windows showing the latest craze,
A lost visitor wearing a frown,
Why do people like the town?

Susy Stark (12)
King Henry VIII School

SUMMER AS WE KNOW IT

Birds chirp
while wind blows through the trees,
the fresh sound of summer breeze,
mothers gardening, children playing,
hearts opening, people saying
how much summer means to them.

When I think of summer
I think of the sun,
it's the time of year when everyone has fun.
No one upset, and no one sad,
no one angry and no one mad.

This is summer as we know it.

Laura Rice (11)
King Henry VIII School

ANOTHER DAY

Boys shout,
Girls giggle,
Pencils write,
Squiggle, squiggle,
Get it wrong,
Bell's gone!
All out!

Balls bounce,
Hands clap,
Skipping ropes,
Slap, slap.
Handstands
By the wall,
Sara Williams
Best of all
Boys fight,
Girls flee,
Teacher's gone
And spilt
His tea!

Clatter, bang!
Big din!
Whistle goes
All in!

All quiet,
No sound,
Hear worms,
Underground.
Chalk squeaks,
Clock creeps,
Head on desk,
Boy sleeps.

Home time!
Glory be!
Mum's got
Chips for tea.
Warm fire,
Full belly,
Sit down,
Watch telly.

Bedtime,
Creep away,
Dream until
Another day.

Christina Watson (11)
King Henry VIII School

ME

My name is Robert
but my friends call me Rob,
my hair is brown
and I've got a fish called Bob.

I like rounders, footy and swimming,
my favourite stroke is front crawl.
I have lots of fun playing with a football.
I have a brother, a sister,
a mum and dad,
sometimes they can make me mad.

I've a lot of friends
they are a lot of fun,
the best thing to do with your mates
is playing in the sun.

Robert Peacock (11)
King Henry VIII School

WHAT I DO EVERYDAY

I get up and feed the cat
get the milk off the mat

I go in the shower
I only take a quarter of an hour

Get dressed
my hair is a mess

My sister is calling
while I'm still yawning

I go to school
feeling cool

After the day is done
I come home for some fun

It's time for bed
another day ahead.

Hannah James (11)
King Henry VIII School

GRAN, CAN YOU RAP?

Gran was in her chair.
She was taking a nap.
So I tapped her on the shoulder
To see if she could rap.
Then she opened one eye
And said to me,
'Man, I'm the best rapping gran,
This world has ever seen!
I'm tip-tap-slip-slop-rap-rap queen!'

Luke Courtney-Hart (11)
King Henry VIII School

WITCHES

Witches
Oh witches
They give you a fright,
You think they're going to come in the night.

They wear pointy hats,
They have a pointy nose
And wear a big cloak.

Witches
Oh witches
They give you a fright,
You think they're going to come in the night.

Rhys Dawe (12)
King Henry VIII School

MY DOG PIPPA

She is so lovely,
My dog Pippa
She runs
She jumps
She chases rabbits and catches flies

She is so lovely,
My dog Pippa
She is black
She is white
Her tail wags and her nose is wet
She is so lovely,
My dog Pippa.

Francis Tomlins (12)
King Henry VIII School

OH NO!

'Oh no! Oh no!
I walk too slow
And now I'm late for school.'

'Oh dear! Oh dear!
I say with fear
Because I trip and feel a fool.'

'Oh spite! Oh spite!
My top's not tight -
I've broken a fashion rule.'

The above are just
Some of the fears
A rich schoolgirl might dread
But let's now look
At some of the fears
A poor African girl might've said.

'Oh no! Oh no!
My poor brother, Joe
He's so weak, he'll probably die.'

'Oh dear! Oh dear!
It's so hot this year
I fetch water as our throats are so dry.'

'Oh spite! Oh spite!
I'm filled with fright,
My family's starving and I start to cry.'

The above are just
Some of the fears
A poor African girl might dread.
Now think of your fears
And compare the two girls
And consider what I've said.

Mari Davies (12)
King Henry VIII School

MY SCHOOL MORNING

Oh how I love the weekend
Nothing to do all day
No homework or anything
It's paradise this way.

Then! Monday comes, school again
Up early, have a shower and a wash
Breakfast is cornflakes,
Lunch is crisps, sarnies, chocolate and squash.

On the way to school
Past the Londis get a snack
Blast, forget my lunch on the kitchen table.
Run home and put it in my backpack.

Running like mad now
About 50 miles per hour
Straight ahead, round the corner
Getting tired, I'm running out of power.

Lotti Jones (12)
King Henry VIII School

FOOTBALL

Football is one of my favourite sports,
No funny business of tracks or courts.
Into the net the ball will go,
The score 1-0, the big board shows.
Football is one of my favourite games,
All those T-shirts titled with names.
The players are tired, there's one half to go till the end,
Here comes the ball, are they ready to defend?
Faster and faster the ball gains speed,
Two more points needed to become in the lead.
The score is now 1-1,
The game is almost done,
Twenty seconds on the clock,
Spectators watching, mouths open in shock,
The game is done,
The reds have won!
There's a cheer from the crowd,
Oh so very loud!
As the team go to celebrate
The cheering fans leave at the gate.

Robyn Taylor (13)
King Henry VIII School

RABBITS

Rabbits are small
But some are tall
Their tails are
Like cotton balls

My rabbit is very clever
He scratches the shed door
He really likes his food
He always comes back for more

He always follows me around
He squeezes through the gate
And if he gets lost
It puts me in a state.

Teresa Bruton (12)
King Henry VIII School

BUDDIES

Yo, my name is Ellie
My bestest buddie is Callie
We both love shopping and singing
We hate most boys, they're minging!

My favourite colour is baby blue
But I don't care if you don't like it too
I love to have my buddies sleep over
I am so glad that they don't live in Dover!

I met a new friend in secondary school
Her name is Lucy and she's kinda cool
She loves her horses, she even has two
I wonder if her hobbie with horses is new!

I love to watch EastEnders and other soaps
I go to dance but we don't hang from ropes
My favourite pop stars are Pink and the Kittens
My friend Amy has a cat called Mittens!

I have a football crazy friend and she hangs with all the boys
Her name is Yas, she's grown out of all her toys
I have three other friends, Bridie, Amy and Laura . . .

They are the best buddies
I could wish for and more!

Ellie Deering (11)
King Henry VIII School

THE COLOURS OF THE RAINBOW

Red is the colour of our runny blood
It is also the colour of our wet lips,
Red is the colour of yummy jam
It is also the colour of a hot chilli pepper.

Yellow is the colour of our boiling sun
It is also the colour of tall sunflowers,
Yellow is the colour of hard sweetcorn
It is also the colour of melting butter.

Pink is the colour of my friend's pencil case
It is also the colour of smelly pigs,
It is also the colour of strawberry milkshake
It is also the colour of my sister's Barbie.

Green is the colour of lush, cool grass
It is also the colour of fresh mint,
Green is the colour of a tree lizard
It is also the colour of garden peas.

Orange is the colour of fresh oranges
It is also the colour of my pencil case,
Orange is the colour of flowers in gardens
It is also the colour of a summer's evening.

Purple is the colour of a funny snake
It is also the colour of grapes,
Purple is the colour of my bedroom
It is also the colour of my furry diary.

Lucy Blowfield (11)
King Henry VIII School

HAVE YOU EVER WONDERED?

Have you ever wondered?
On a clear night's sky,
What are the stars?
How? When? And why?

How did they get there?
When were they born?
And why are some brighter
In the early morn?

Have you ever wondered?
When out at sea,
What's under the surface?
What might you see?

A strange new creature?
An old treasury
Or maybe even,
A great, lost city?

Have you ever wondered?
Why do you wonder?
What makes you think?
What makes you ponder?

The amazing brain,
Inside your head,
Seeking knowledge, even when,
You're dreaming in bed.

Rory Wesson (12)
King Henry VIII School

MOTHER

My name for God,
You've always been there,
Through good times and bad,
Thinking of me before anything else,
What did I do to deserve you?
When times were good you were there
To encourage me, to be proud of me.
When times were bad you were there
To help me - a shoulder to cry on.
When I felt alone in the world,
You consoled me when no one could.
Every path I take, you guide me,
Nudging me in the right direction.
Every day I think of you,
You're a mother to be proud of,
Always appreciated, always loved.
Could I have come this far without you?
If depression was in my world,
One word from you would bring joy.
You are my guiding star,
My angel,
My god,
My mother.

James Woods (13)
King Henry VIII School

MY POEM

Shakira is the name of my dog.
The colour of her is black and white,
She likes to chew on a log
Never ever has to bite.

She plays with the boys,
I take her for long walks,
Has got lots of toys,
Don't think she will ever talk!

Stacey Price (11)
King Henry VIII School

SCHOOL DRUELS

Art makes me mad,
RE drives me nuts,
Science makes me bored
And
So do all the rest.
English makes me sleepy,
History wakes me up,
Music makes me daft
And
So do all the rest.
Technology drives me bonkers,
IT drives me up the wall
And
So do all the rest.
But wait for just one more,
Geography is hell-like,
I really mean it
And
It drives me nuts, mad, bored,
Sleepy, daft, bonkers
And
So do all the rest!

Dale Williams (12)
King Henry VIII School

THE COUNTRY

In the country there are wild flowers,
The flowers are beautiful,
They are all different colours, shapes and sizes,
The colours are blues, greens, pinks and all other lovely colours,
The flowers smell of perfume and feel like velvet between your fingers.

Bunnies that bounce here and there,
Foxes wandering at night to find food for their families,
Birds flying overhead,
Birds of prey looking down and diving for treats,
Squirrels skipping up trees so they can store their nuts for winter.

The cows in the farm are being milked
So when you have some milk you have a white moustache,
Horses in the fields eating the crunchy, chewy grass
With the foals sucking the rich milk from their mothers,
The young horses galloping up and down the long fields,
Pigs in barns honking at the farmer waiting for their food.

Giselle Quarrington (12)
King Henry VIII School

EARTH

E   arth is our home planet
A   nd we should be proud of it.
R   ock solid plates of stone are under the surface of the land.
T   he Earth is exactly the same shape as a ball (a sphere).
H   ot molten lava comes form the centre of Earth.

Benjamin Townley (11)
King Henry VIII School

SEASONS

The time is winter and the nights are cold,
The snow is falling and the year is growing old.
The robin chirps, such a sweet song,
The winter is where all these things belong.

The time is spring, all fresh and new,
Flowers start blooming yellow and blue.
The lambs are leaping on the farm,
While the chicks are pecking in the barn.

The time is summer, the days are getting longer,
The heat from the sun is growing stronger.
We play games in the park,
Almost until it's completely dark.

The time is autumn, harvest has come,
We pick an apple, a pear, a plum.
The leaves are falling off the trees,
Floating in the gentle breeze.

Nathan Collins (11)
King Henry VIII School

A BOY CALLED OWEN

Once there was a boy called Owen,
He said to his mum, 'I'm going.
I'm going to play on my bike as much as I like!'
And that's the end of the poem!

Owen West (11)
King Henry VIII School

Y FENNI

My house is in Abergavenny,
Which Welsh people call Y Fenni.
Welsh is a funny language,
I don't know how I manage it.
Bore da and Sut wyt ti?
What's that?

I moved here, to Abergavenny
Which Welsh people call Y Fenni
Three years ago from London.
At first I didn't like it,
Till one day Dad said,
'Follow me!' and lead
Me up the tall, tall Skirrid.
We got to the top and looked down
I couldn't see a single town.
Just patchwork quilt, the biggest I've ever seen!
It was all green
It rolled on and on and on and on and on forever!

My house is in Abergavenny
Welsh people say Y Fenni
Now I love it here.
Sadly we are moving back to London next year.
One day I'll come back to Abergavenny
Which Welsh people call Y Fenni
And the hills roll on and on and on and on forever.

Emily Wright (11)
King Henry VIII School

US TEENAGERS

Our parents think they're always right,
We cheek them back and have a shouting fight,
Our bedrooms have to be spotlessly clean,
Otherwise we're grounded, parents are so mean!
They never want us to go out,
It really annoys me I have to pout,
Parents give us lectures on things we have to do,
I daydream and fall asleep too.
When you gossip to your friends on the phone,
Parents ask you what you're talking about and moan,
You tell a lie and go along with it all day,
They tell you that they know, but I still won't say.
I'm in the bath for an hour,
They tell me to get out,
I wash my hair under water,
I can still hear them shout!
When you get your pocket money
And buy something cool,
They tell you to save,
But who's going to listen to that, you?

Overall parents are good
And look after us like they should,
It'd be great if they'd listen to us,
But hey, we can all dream!

Kim Brown (12)
King Henry VIII School

ME AND MY FRIENDS

I am Callie and wanna go far,
I have four best friends and here they are.
Ellie, Bridie, Amy, Yasmine,
They all have hobbies and they are;
Ellie likes singing and Bridie does too,
Amy and Yasmine come and join the crew.

We all love singing very loud,
Just in front of a very big crowd,
We all have blue eyes except for Ellie,
I think it's because she's obsessed with the tele.

We all made a promise to be best friends forever,
I hope you like my poem, it's very, very clever.

Callie Jones (11)
King Henry VIII School

CHRISTMAS!

Christmas is the time of year where families meet together.
They give presents and gifts which we treasure forever
With sparkly lights and all things nice.
Santa Claus has a big fat belly!
All he does is watch the telly,
But when it comes Christmas time
He will re-enact this Christmas rhyme.

Bridie Horler (11)
King Henry VIII School

THE HOUSE

That house on windy hill
'Tis said to be haunted
So me and my mate went up there one day
And boy did we regret it.

The first sign came when we saw her face
Her face was white and cold
But we still went in
Then a scream, a horrible scream made me shiver all over.

Then we saw it, zombies awaken.
We ran as fast as we could
Out of that horrid house . . .

Daniel Goodall (12)
King Henry VIII School

MY FAMILY

My mum is nice as pie,
My brother he always cries.

My best friend likes to sing,
My sister has got four rings.

My cat is in the tree,
My dog always jumps on me.

My dad is really crazy,
My grandad doesn't like gravy.

And me? I'm just perfect.

Dayna Thomas (14)
King Henry VIII School

FOOTBALL WORLD

Man United
Everyone watch Man U roar,
You never know when Dave might score.
They sprint and pass everywhere,
Whenever they do it, they don't care.
But when Man U start to fail,
The crowd are there, they start to wail.

World Cup
Come on people, watch them play,
Before you come in you have to pay.
Who's the team that wins the cup,
You want to know, suggest you shut up.
Could be Ireland,
Could be England,
But the team that wins is . . . Brazil!

Rhys Fury (11)
King Henry VIII School

RIVERS

Rivers are like people,
They change in so many ways,
A person's mood changes throughout the day.
One minute they're angry, the next sad, happy then insane.
Rivers are the same,
One minute they are slow, elegant,
Things trickling over sticks and stones,
Next they are violent, putting you in danger zones,
But sometimes rivers and people are different.
Have you seen that rivers tend to go on forever
Where as people slow down, stop, give up. the end!

Rosie Powell (12)
King Henry VIII School

PS2

One green eye,
One blue eye,
You have black skin,
You are very thin.
I think I'm in love,
Please don't leave me,
My PlayStation 2.

You bring entertainment into the world,
If you are gone, the world will be cold,
So stay and make people happy.
In this world gone soppy,
If you go,
Who will know
What to do without you,
My PlayStation 2?

William Jones (12)
King Henry VIII School

HALLS OF THE BLIND

I can see what you see not,
Vision milky than eyes rot,
When you turn they will be gone,
Whispering their hidden song,
Then you see what cannot be,
Darkness moves where light should be,
Out of darkness, out of mind,
Lost down into the halls of the blind.

James Luke (12)
King Henry VIII School

REASONS

A graceful canter across the moors,
Hungry heads over the stable doors,
Long manes flowing in the breeze,
Thick winter coats so they don't freeze.

Horses for ploughing, working all day,
Others at rest, munching on hay.
Proud, strong mares with foals at foot,
The father, a stallion, as black as soot.

Polo ponies display speed and pace,
Dressage horses show beauty and grace,
Racehorses thunder away from the start,
Cheeky bay Shetlands pull a small cart.

Showjumpers elegantly enter the ring
Cantering circles, awaiting the 'ding.'
Eventers show courage out on the course,
These are the reasons why I love the horse.

Jenny Marshall (13)
King Henry VIII School

THE HOUSE ON THE HILL

There's an old house on that old hill.
There's an old house that still keeps its will.
There's an old house with dusty windows.
There's an old house with chimney cinders.
There's an old house with a creaky door.
There's an old house with no carpeted floor.
There's an old house with a widow inside.
There's an old man from there who somehow died.

James Townley (12)
King Henry VIII School

THE RAINFOREST

Rainforest sensations are all around me,
water slowly drips onto my head.
I'm totally astounded, they're cutting it down
and distributing wood everywhere.

Rainforest sounds are drowned out
by the roar of monstrous machines.
I'm totally astounded, they're cutting it down
and distributing wood everywhere.

Rainforest scents overpower my nostrils
but are soon trampled down by the rubbery tarmac.
I'm totally astounded, they're cutting it down
and distributing the wood everywhere.

No more rainforest sensations surround me,
no more water drips heavily down,
no more scents overpower my nostrils.
They cut it all down,
the rainforest is no more.

Kate Mills (13)
King Henry VIII School

THINGS CHANGE

Plants change, they grow and die,
Houses change, walls get knocked down and built,
The sky changes from light to dark and dark to light.
Things like shoes wear out,
Rubbish rots.
We change!
But they say a leopard never changes his spots.

Maisie Noble (11)
King Henry VIII School

SNOWY NIGHT

Walking home from Grandad's
On a dark and snowy night,
The mountains were blanketed
The view was a lovely sight.

My little dog Bella
Is as white as the snow,
I love her tremendously
But does she love me, that's what I want to know.

As we were walking home
Bella's neat footsteps behind,
We saw a creepy shadow
That made us want to hide.

We were nearly home
Five minutes to go,
It seemed like forever
I couldn't wait, you know.

Finally we were home
Hot chocolate just for me,
My mother asked why I was late
But it wasn't meant to be.

I said goodnight to my mother
And gave her a kiss on the cheek,
Then went upstairs and tucked into bed
And then fell fast asleep.

Katie McCarthy (12)
King Henry VIII School

MY PETS

Cadbury's my dog,
that's what she does,
she lies there all day,
dreaming away.
Other times she is totally different,
she pounces and plays all day long,
when she's in trouble, she knows she's wrong.

Lulu's my cat,
she's extremely fat,
she lies on the boiler all day,
not moving away.
Other times she is totally different,
she's miaowing and scratching at the door,
as if she's begging,
like someone poor.

Arnie's the kitten,
in the morning he hides behind the hoover
and when you walk past,
he's on your leg,
he's a quick mover.
Other times he is totally different,
when he's tired he curls up into a fluffy heap
sleeping away behind the sofa seat.

Livvy Martin (13)
King Henry VIII School

SEASONS

Holidays come in summer,
A time when there's no school,
No need to wear a jumper,
Instead go in the paddling pool.

Baby lambs are born,
Dew lies on the ground,
Fields are full of corn,
Children sleep sound as sound.

Warm colours fill the air,
Golden, crisp leaves blow in gales,
Seeing green is very rare,
Hay's harvested into bales.

Snow is fluffy and white,
Night comes during the day,
Jack Frost is ready to bite,
Christmas is here - wish it would stay.

Lizzie Stroud (12)
King Henry VIII School

SIEGFRIED

I have a kitten called Siegfried,
But we all call him 'Seaweed'
He's ginger and white and fluffy too,
Except his paws when he's been to the loo.

He sleeps on a cushion, fluffy and blue
And times when he's off it are rare and few,
He thinks the cushion is his mummy cat
And pummels and pushes until it is flat.

Eight inches long is his tail,
Yet he only walks as fast as a snail,
Oh Seaweed you are a lovely boy,
Much better than any toy.

Peter Baldwin-Jones (11)
King Henry VIII School

FISHING

Fishing is great fun.
It's great when you get up before
The sun, sitting there beside my mate.

We compete all day, which is great
Fun to see who catches the biggest fish,
Changing bait and throwing it out.

And waiting for that float to go
Under, striking with tremendous speed
And bringing the fish in and putting it in
The keepnet, then with even more speed
Putting the bait on and doing it all over again.

Then when we have had enough we get
All our things together and pack up and off we go.
But before all that we put the fish we caught
Back in the pond and watch them swim off
To where they came from
To be caught again by someone else.

Adam Gailis (15)
King Henry VIII School

LIFE OR DEATH

Warm and cosy in my den,
What's that noise?
Oh no, not again!

Here they come,
Galloping near
Now I begin to really fear.

I begin to panic
And start to run
Oh dear, dear, this is no fun.

I can feel their breath
Upon my brush
Keep on going rush, rush, rush.

I'm in the farmer's field of long grass
Perhaps if I'm careful they will pass.

My plan has worked and I've doubled back,
Only to find another pack.

My time is up so I'll say goodbye,
But ten against one is pretty sly.

James Silverthorne (13)
King Henry VIII School

THUNDER AND LIGHTNING

A crack of thunder in the night
A blast of light causes fright.

Electric shocks in the clouds
Bright lights fill the sky.

Thunder sounds like a lion's roar
As the heaven's waters pour.

Lock up the animals and the little children
Hear comes the big one.

Thomas House (12)
King Henry VIII School

WHY?

I get up in the morning,
Wander down the street,
Humming an attractive tune,
Feet tapping to the New York beat.

But then I hear a deadly crash
And see a fiery cloud
Smoke and rubble come my way
So do a screaming crowd.

I run to my house,
Scared and shocked
Try the door,
But find it locked.

As I attempt to
Find my key,
Pray that someone
Is watching over me.

It's September the 11th,
I look into the sky
So many deaths in one day,
I just wonder why?

Kathryn Prothero (12)
King Henry VIII School

ON THAT NIGHT!

On that night wondering why
A spacecraft came drifting by,
I stopped, I stared, I mean what a sight!

The flashing lights and bright coloured lights,
A screech of fear, oh no, it's getting nearer!

The   s
        t
        a
        i
        r
        s   unfold and slowly walks a creepy
                    figure covered in mould.

Two bright eyes as big as kites
Ten sharp teeth, that might just bite.

I start to run but that's not much fun,
So I stop and munch on a bun.

The beady eyes began to roll as he
Saw the bun and began to run.

I let the bun lead the great north chase,
When suddenly he had taken my case.

I ran and ran, trying to catch that beast,
When I saw a funny sort of light
High in the sky at night
Two figures started to wave
One was big, one was small.

I said, 'Goodbye and let's all sleep, nice and tight.'
Morning comes and I'm still yawning
But where's the bun and the alien?

Maddy White (12)
King Henry VIII School

MUSIC TO END WITH

Know no fears
The band still plays
Oncoming rage
Our way it steers
A bassist bold, a drummer untold
A microphone wielded never more brave
Stand against certain death
Sing out your final breath
Stars crash down
But the band still plays.

Apocalypse, four horsemen come not near
The world will die, but not yet, not here.
That beat will break my body
A rhythm to send me crazy
God takes what He needs
Says goodbye to His creation
Then leaves them to fend
Against the destruction
And on through flames
The band still plays.

His solo, never before and never again
Noise of death ignored
Screams of love over screams of pain
The world listens on
All sorrow and anguish is past
Ground crumbles underfoot
Then at last
The end of life and end of Earth
But echoed in memories
The band still plays.

Michael Addis (13)
King Henry VIII School

A HOPELESS CAUSE

A dark, dreary October dawn,
The dew lies fresh on the open lawn.
My friend lost in hope and dream,
A girl passes by his wonder queen.

Days pass by, he stands and stares,
To chance a kiss he wouldn't dare.
Like a nut in a nutshell, so helpless he feels,
Afraid to tell, afraid to squeal.

Oh, with what wonder he looks upon her face,
Fighting, ever fighting to exhaust her and embrace.
Oh, what a pity, he never had a chance,
She fell in love with another soul with a short, single glance.

With this fateful tragedy, he walks off in a shot,
Leaving his poor heart, tied up in simple knots.
He bowed his head and walked off in shame,
He made me promise never to tell his name.

Jonathan Worgan (12)
King Henry VIII School

THE SEEKER

By the sea
near the shore
on the rocks
lives someone poor.

Across the land
beyond the fort
lies a village
the rich bought.

Through the farms
past the hills
no fields of corn
the land lies still.

The world changes
the Earth spins
planets align
the sun dims.

Aneirin Jones (11)
King Henry VIII School

THE FAIR

It's a Friday night and the fair's in town,
I love the rides that go up and down.
The feeling in your belly when you freefall,
It's the top of the lot, best of them all.

When the fair had stopped and packed away,
I went to the park and there I stayed.
It was freaky and dark, I know,
But I was too scared to go home.

In the park, in the park all on my own,
It's freaky and scary and I'm scared to go home.
I could get raped or taken away,
Anything could happen today.

I woke up in the morning, all wet and cold,
The police soon found me and wouldn't listen to the story I told.

Louise-Amy Sheppard (13)
King Henry VIII School

SCHOOL'S A FOOL

Hi, my name is Paul
I'm not very tall
I go to school
Which ain't too cool
I'd rather be by a pool
Than be in school
I don't like the rules
That they give me in school.

In school I study
IT and RE
Go back in time in history
All this in King Henry
They keep me busy
Which really gets me
I would rather be free
Than at King Henry.

Sometimes it bugs me
The homework they give me
I have no time to be free
To be me
Weekend I study
For English and geography
I think it's time they gave me
Time away from King Henry!

Only three years to go
Which will go slow
On the dole I'll go
Unless the line I toe
My future I will blow
No money will flow
So King Henry I will stay
And pass, I pray.

Paul Symonds (13)
King Henry VIII School

SNOW IS THE BEST

S   now is the best
N   o one can deny that
O   h so cold
W   inter is cool

I   ce and snow
S   now and ice

T   rue?
H   ow does it snow?
E   verybody wonders

B   rr, it's cold
E   verybody says
S   tart snowing . . .
T   onight

Snow is the best!

Lauren Richards (12)
King Henry VIII School

WAR HAS ERUPTED

War has erupted
I have been abducted
The aliens and me are as happy as can be.

I've lost my mum
I've lost my dad
I am a poor, neglected lad.

Eye of the tiger, not afraid to attack
Left Frankenstein flat on his back
In war there ain't nothing to see
And everyone is free.

There is no good news in war
Except for the people that win.
Victory!

Jessica Hill (13)
King Henry VIII School

THE SEA

Wild, calm, blue and green,
an underwater world rarely seen.
Coral reefs, shipwrecks and caves,
all mysteriously hidden by the waves.
Strange creatures live within the deep,
what secrets do these waters keep?

Unexplained happenings of sailors' tales,
of these sea creatures and big white whales.
Exciting, ferocious, tamed and free,
all captured by the waves of the sea.

Bradley Webb (11)
King Henry VIII School

I WOULDN'T MIND . . .

I wouldn't mind being a tree
Yes, I really would like being a tree.

I could then stand on a field just by myself
And think of how the wind blows through my leaves.

I wouldn't mind being a stone
Yes, I really would like being a stone.

I could then lay down on the beach just by myself
And think how the waves run over me.

I wouldn't mind being the sea,
Yes, I really would like being the sea.
I could then be everywhere
And think of how the storm goes through me . . .

Edith Gustafsson (13)
King Henry VIII School

SUBARU WRX

The car that I like is one of a kind,
No hassle, no bother, it's one of a kind,
With blue paint and gold alloys, no wonder Makkinen drives it.

The engine revving and speedometer whizzing,
It's surely one of a kind with anti-lag popping
And turbo kicking, it's surely one of a kind.

He races in the rallies to get that prize,
The prize of winning the WRC,
So he puts all her power in it, just to get to that turbo.

Owen Thompson (12)
King Henry VIII School

BONFIRE NIGHT

It is cold outside on Bonfire Night,
With different colours in the sky,
The fire is blazing, warm and bright.
While fireworks dart out way up high,
People huddle round the fire as
The flames leap higher and higher,
Guy Fawkes sits upon the top
Limp and lank until he flops.

Excited children bravely hold
Twinkling sparklers in the cold,
Hot dogs on sale for all to buy
Dripping with ketchup and onions - fried!
Toffee apples crunchy and crisp,
Munched between hungry lips,
Roman Candles suddenly flare
Lights and colour everywhere.

As the fire fades away
Fireworks from the huge display
Settle down among the ashes,
No more bangs or booms or crashes.
Quietly we make our way
Happy with the passing day,
Mum and Dad hold both my hands
They make me feel safe and sound!

Lydia Frost (15)
King Henry VIII School

BLACK CATS ARE GOOD LUCK

I have a furry kitten
He's only one week old
He is black all over
His eyes they shine like gold.

Miaow is all he says
He really won't shut up!
But I still love him anyway
After all he brings good luck.

Louise Alldred (13)
King Henry VIII School

THE TREE

Standing tall and proud
above the evergreen crowd,
the ancient oak watches the world go by
as it grows ever greater towards the sky.

Spring has arrived
and the tree is alive
with crawling bugs and slithery slugs
and bees in and out of their hives.

This really is a city with comings and goings
the birds in their nests
and the acorns are growing
into future rests.

Soon the winter comes,
wind, snow and rain,
the leaves are all gone
but it will be spring again.

The tree will come alive
and the cycle will begin,
the birds in the branches
will sing, sing, sing.

Karl Pendry (12)
King Henry VIII School

CHILDHOOD

When I was young, life seemed such fun,
I used to play out nearly every day,
Until the sun went down and the night went glum.

Then came winter, snowballs and sledges,
Trees with no leaves and stripped, bare hedges,
The days seemed so short, the nights were cold,
So I stayed in watch TV until another early night fell in.

Then came crèche time,
Making new friends and having a laugh,
Days went so quick then, now it's in the past.

Soon came school,
The reception class waited,
Suddenly my past seemed so dated,
This was my childhood.

Tobi Wilding (14)
King Henry VIII School

ONE COLD NIGHT

One cold night when the sky was dark,
I hard the cry of an injured lark.

The cry was shrill, the cry was loud,
I could feel the presence of a darkening cloud.

And as the chill of the night reared its ugly head,
The lark fell silent into its everlasting bed.

Michelle Williams (11)
King Henry VIII School

THE NEWSPAPER FAIRY

She flits about to get the paper done on time,
She's the one that makes poems rhyme.
Who makes the paper look alright?
Writes stories guaranteed to give a fright!
She isn't horrid, green or hairy
She's the amazing, wonderful newspaper fairy.
Who gets the one amazing photo,
While riding on her dog called Toto!
The newspaper world wouldn't be the same
If they didn't have that fairy brain
She's not horrid, green or hairy
She's the amazing, wonderful newspaper fairy.

Louise Brown (14)
King Henry VIII School

GONE FISHING

Getting up early on a misty day
Packing my kit, then on my way
I go down to the river without making a sound
Set up my stuff, then sit on the ground
I set up my rod and put on the bait
Cast into the water and sat there to wait
I sit there waiting to catch a sight
Of the fish coming to take the bite.
The day is now over, so I reel the line in
And set off home without a single thing.

Luke Shaw (16)
King Henry VIII School

HAVE YOU EVER WONDERED?

Have you ever wondered what's beyond the moon?
Wouldn't you like to go there soon?
See the planets, the moons and the sun,
Wouldn't it be so much fun?

In the future, who knows we might,
Fly in a spaceship faster than light.
Or perhaps we'll fly past the stars,
In our convertible flying cars?

Wouldn't it be great to be an astronaut?
To explore things of our wildest thoughts;
Floating around with no gravity,
Or just staring at stars with joy and glee.

Do you think there's life on Mars,
Jupiter, Venus or past the stars?
Do you think they'll be big, scary things,
Or friendly and cheerful that laugh and sing?

I'd love to meet one, friendly or mean,
But if they're dangerous, I won't be so keen;
I'd teach them to speak perfect English,
For it to come back to Earth would be my wish.

Space is something we need to explore,
So we can find out a lot more;
I want to go there, it would be great
To explore all this, I just can't wait.

Kate Jones (13)
King Henry VIII School

INNOCENT LIVES ARE TAKEN

(This poem is a true story, which I took from the newspaper and made into a poem. It's about a man called Leonard Farrar)

Leonard Farrar lived his life protectively
Scared and frightened of any thief,
He cared for his life and house securely
But he still lived with great grief.

A normal chap and a retired cabbie
The neighbours said he was a lovely guy,
Formerly always cheerful and happy
But sadly he got murdered and died.

It was a lovely, warm Saturday night
Him alone with his good wife,
Until some burglars gave them a fright
Leonard fought and struggled for his life.

Len was never to give any trouble
But he still got stabbed, dead in the hall,
Lying there helpless like a pile of rubble
Chances of finding the killers are small.

The entire neighbourhood complained
That there were never any police around,
So they finally decided to make a campaign
But still no bobbies were to be found.

These victims are piling up, queue by queue
The killers are not getting caught,
It's because they have nothing good to do
And a firm lesson has to be taught.

Amrit Bhatia (13)
King Henry VIII School

THE WORLD IS YOUR BLANKET

The world is your blanket,
So snuggle up tight,
The world is your blanket,
High as a kite.

The world is our mother,
Love and pain,
God we just love her,
But what do we gain?

Water and land,
The world is our home,
Sunsets and sand,
Why do we moan?

War ad peace,
Gunfire and woe,
The world's on a leash,
Everybody says, oh no.

The world stops,
Mary and Joseph,
And then it pops
We have religion.

Love the world
And all that's in it,
Are friendships pearled,
Get out of the pit.

Katie Moss (13)
King Henry VIII School

THE BLACK KNIGHT

When the Black Knight
Comes out at night,
He'll ride and ride
Through the thick, black night.
He'll catch his prey
Like an eagle in the day,
He will stalk and stalk
Like the ghost of his hawk.

As he rides into the mist
The people insist, he shall be caught
The next time he stalks.

Joseph Davey (11)
King Henry VIII School

LIKE A FIG TO ITS TREE

As thoughts within may be dull and grim,
Outside is a life of happiness,
Let people know or your bad feelings will grow
To a life that is dark and scary.
So stand up to your problem, like a fig to its tree,
For the power is great, but little and lies deep within me.
Be strong and courageous with a smile on your face
Because the battle is already won.

Abby Dullea (11)
King Henry VIII School

BOMBS FALLING GRACEFULLY

A brilliant, blue sky, sun slowly rising above the horizon,
Its radiant colours glowing a mixture of yellow, red and orange.
The waves of the turquoise sea below breaking on the rocks,
The vision and reality of waking up on a beautiful
Sunday morning into hectic hell.

Fighter planes buzzing through the sky like a huge, hungry swarm of
bees, making their way over to the sea's harbour,
where nearly 300 sitting ducks were at port.
100s, 1000s of tons of bombs being dropped into the sea.
There was no longer a tranquil, turquoise but a raging, bloody blue.

Hospitals packed, the kitchens in use to make way for dead, dying men.
'You're going to be alright, you're going to survive.'
The nurses and doctors would say, knowing full well to drug them with
morphine to make sure they survived their horrors.

Heroic men dying in combat for their country, on a kind of mission
from which they knew full well that their medals would be sent to the
family.

Rhian Price (13)
King Henry VIII School

MY MUM

My mum is kind, my mum is sweet
My mum is there for me when things go wrong
I love you Mum for who you are
You brought me up and made me who I am.

You're there for me when I need you most
Even when I get in my moods
When I'm stubborn or even upset
You're always there for me.

I love you Mum, I want you to know
How much I really love you so
You are so kind and so sweet
I'm glad I've got a mum like you.

I hope you know I'll always be
There for you too
Just like you are there for me
And that's the way it's gonna be.

Emily Thomas (13)
King Henry VIII School

DAYDREAMS

The teacher is droning on and on,
I have no idea what about.
Anyway, why should it be,
Of any importance to me?

So instead I gaze out of the window,
Wishing I was anywhere but here.
I rest my head in my hands and sigh,
What fun I could have if I could fly.

If I could fly, I'd sail out of the room,
Into the world outside.
I would fly up and up, far away,
I'd never have to listen to what Miss Jones had to say.

I only have one life to live,
Does it have to be this dull?
I don't seem to have much choice,
I just have to listen to her dreary old voice!

Emily Pritchard (12)
King Henry VIII School

FOOTBALL

I play 90 minutes every Sunday
I train Tuesday and Thursday
I woke up late on the day
To find out that we were playing away
I had to rush
To get the bus.

We got there just before kick-off
We didn't have time to train
We thought we were going to be in pain.

They were all over us
We might as well get back on the bus
But we hit them on the counter attack
Our goal was scored by John Mack
1-0 to us, we were getting better
And it was getting wetter.

Half-time came, we were 1-0 up
We thought we were going to win the cup
The second half started
After Gezza parted
They came at us
Without a fuss
Before we knew it
We had blown it
1-1 was the score
We needed to attack more
The last minute of the game
The score was the same.
We got a free kick
We couldn't pick
Who was going to score the final goal.

Gareth Williams (14)
King Henry VIII School

SCHOOL DAYS

School days, long and boring,
Could be at home watching TV,
Have to go, Mum says so,
Oh why do I have to get up so early?

Off I go on the long road to school,
Stuck behind a granny going really slow,
Unlucky for us we get overtaken by a bus,
We're coming close to school now.

Mr Kendrick teaching us history first,
Stuarts, no Tudors that's what we're learning,
All about some battle,
How boring.

Love English though,
Our teacher's the best,
All I hope is I don't fail my next
Test!

Matthew Dilley (12)
King Henry VIII School

HEAVEN SENT

There once was a man from Devon
Who tried to swim the Severn
In less than an hour
He turned a bit sour
And now he is in Heaven.

Rebecca Mapp (11)
King Henry VIII School

BEGGING FOR MONEY - WISHING FOR LOVE

He sits there by the corner shop
    Surrounded by plastic bags
His beard is tangled and matted
    In his anorak and rags.

He gazes at pedestrians
    Who bustle down the street
Wishing for their comfy shoes
    To warm his freezing feet.

Although he begs for money
    He desires something more
He wishes for some love and care
    As he sits there on the floor.

Genevieve Jones (12)
King Henry VIII School

RAIN

It pitter-patters on the floor,
It pitter-patters at the door,

It flows down the drain
But when it's blocked it runs down the lane.

It makes everything wet
And everyone cold I bet.

When it's dry and then it rains,
It makes everyone slip in pain.

Overall the rain is great
But it can lead to someone's fate.

Tara Lewis (12)
King Henry VIII School

OLD AGE

As you start to age and age,
Your book of life comes to its final page.
You hair might fall out or at least go grey,
You hope to live another day,
You long to be the child you once were,
Who stroked his cat to hear him purr,
You made model planes and played with a tank,
But now you collect your pension from the bank.

You like to read and watch TV,
Thinking of how the world used to be,
Five sweets for a penny and less pollution,
It all just seems like an illusion.

When kids kick their ball in your back garden,
You start to shout and demand a pardon,
Being old just isn't fun,
Because you know your time on Earth is almost done.

Sam Watkins (11)
King Henry VIII School

A THOUGHT OF YOU!

If a raindrop was a kiss
I'd send you a shower,
If a hug was a flower
I'd send you bunches,
If I had a wish,
I'd wish for you,
If love was a person
I'd send you me
But these are just the thoughts I've had of you!

Malinka Stevens (13)
King Henry VIII School

CAT ATTACK

Their long, sleek bodies,
Pad through the spiky hay,
As a fieldmouse scuttles to a berry,
There the cat is eager and ready to pounce,
Like a praying mantis,
He jumps, the mouse panics,
He tries to run, he tries to hide,
Too late, the long, sharp, beak-like earthy claws,
Dig into the warm, soft body,
The head is forced under the canines,
Crunch, the neck breaks.
Blood rushes to the mouth of the mouse,
Then slowly sinks back into place,
One hour later the cat picks the mouse up,
It's cold, it's hard, it now has rigamortis,
The proud cat has hunted and returns home.

Kate Toyer (13)
King Henry VIII School

AUTUMN'S COMING

Autumn's coming, children eager
to get conkers and having fights
when one falls to the ground.
Some people just wait till one falls to their feet.
At home time children throw huge objects up into the tree
trying to get the spiky shell which the conker is installed in
safe and protected for when it falls to the hard ground.
There the tree stands in pain and agony
from the children who throw the huge objects at it,
waiting, waiting for another day to come.

Joshua Charles (11)
King Henry VIII School

The World Of A Fox

Our fur is red, like our blood
The blood they want
Our tails are long, like their guns
The guns they use to shoot us with
Our teeth are sharp, like the dogs
That snap at us.

We hide in our homes
But when they find us
They don't stop until we are dead
What kind of life is this for our cubs?
A life of terror and evil.

We wish they would stop
How would they like to be chased and killed
I have lost many friends
All we want is peace for all us foxes.

Bryony Turnbull (14)
King Henry VIII School

I Am . . .

I am all I see - the trees that the birds nest in.
I am all I hear - the wind whistling past the clouds.
I am all I feel - the snow taught the road.
I am all I taste - I am a nice sandwich.
I am and I remember - I am the rain of a cat.
I am all I've been.
Taste - I am the pencil you write with.
I am all I think - I think I'm a ladybird
But one day I will change.
I am like an elephant because I am big and strong.

Nicola Powell (11)
Llandrindod High School

I AM

I am all I see
I am lazy like my brother, sleeping in his room, while everyone is busy
I am grown up like my mum (an adult).

I am all I hear
I am quiet like the class in school when we're working.
I am loud like my cats when they're squealing for food in the morning.

I am all I feel
I feel the breeze outside, across my face cooling my cheeks
each morning.
I feel the hard concrete touching the end of my shoes.
I feel young like a bird free in the air.

I am all I taste
I taste the fizzy, fuzzy, sour lollipop on my tongue, making me
shiver inside.
I taste the spicy, hot curry in the hall at lunch, and it spices my tongue
up, like mad.

I am all I remember
I remember my holidays with my family when I was young.
I remember all my happy, cosy, Christmases at home.

I am all I've been taught
I have been taught English
I have been taught Welsh.

I am all I think
I think of my family, friends, pets/animals.
I think like a computer.

I am like
I am like a seed but ready to be a flower.

I am the
I am the unknown of the future.

Daniella Jayne Lewis (11)
Llandrindod High School

I AM...

I am all I see,
Green fields, with sheep grazing, with the farmer moving sheep.
I am all I hear,
Birds singing, cows mooing. The farmer shouting to his dogs,
'Come by.'
I am all I feel,
A duvet in the morning, warm and cosy.
I am all I taste,
Of chocolate chips and salt and vinegar.
I am all I remember,
Going to Florida in an aeroplane.
I am all I've been taught,
How to ride my motorbike. 'Pick your feet up,' Dad said.
How to cross the road.
I am all I think,
Going home and watching Nickelodeon.
I am like
A dog, not lazy
But
Full of energy.
I am the
Friendliest boy on Earth.

Aled Price (11)
Llandrindod High School

I AM...

I am all I see.
I see trees, flowers and green grass.

I am all I hear.
I hear rustling of leaves and birds singing in trees.

I am all I feel.
I feel warmth and happiness inside me
Reaching out to grab my soul.

I am all I taste.
I taste happiness all around me and
Thankfulness in the air.

I am all I remember.
I remember when I lived in hell, sadness and sorrow.

I am all I've been taught.
I have been taught to enjoy life, how to walk
And how to add up.

I am all I think.
I think of the good times I have had and
The ones to come.

I am like.
I am like a plane flying around but will run out
Of fuel and crash to the ground.

I am the sun because I am happy and never dull.

James Dobb (11)
Llandrindod High School

I AM...

I am all I see.
Hills and people playing football and a ball flying in the air and girls
Posing for the boys.

I am all I hear.
People shouting, 'Pass the ball here,' and then when they score a goal
The crowd is so loud you can't hear yourself think.

I am all I feel.
A ball coming straight for my goal and *bang* it hits with great power
I can feel the ball hit the net.

I am all I taste.
I taste sweat, real sharp and chips full of salt and turkey drummers.

I am all I remember.
I can remember eating my first plate of chips.
They were lovely and I had another plate.

I am all I've been taught.
I've been taught great jokes and rhymes but the best is maths.

I am all I think.
I think of football like whether I should pass or shoot.

I am like a rabbit about to leap out of a hole and run like mad
But then I run on air and float like the speed of sound.

Liam Ryland (11)
Llandrindod High School

I AM...

I am all I see,
The birds in the sky, girls in huddles
Boys playing football, the world as it revolves around me.
I am all I hear,
Turn that TV down, do your homework,
Have a nice day at school. Children screaming in the playground.
I am all I feel,
The breeze in my face, my sweaty hand after writing all lesson.
Being nervous on the first day of high school.
I am all I taste,
The sweet taste of candyfloss when it first touched my tongue,
The dinner on my plate at tea time.
The ugly taste of mustard on my tongue.
I am all I've been bought,
From walking to writing and to being loving and caring.
I am like a little book in the corner of a bookshop
Sitting there for 11 years, but one day I'll be top of the range
Best story in town.
I am the unknown of the future.

Ceinwen McPhee (11)
Llandrindod High School

SECRETS

Secrets can be whispered in ears.
You have to be quiet so no one else hears.
You can keep them to yourself
Or share them with a friend,
But when a secret's told
The consequences are hard to mend.

Important secrets will never be told.
Secrets can mean more than gold.
They can be big or small,
Short or long.
Keep a secret and you can
Never go wrong.

Lauren Hudson (12)
Llandrindod High School

I AM . . .

I am all I see
I see big rectangle windows, I see children walking around the class.
I am all I hear.
I hear voices in front of me and behind me.
I am all I feel.
I feel a smooth warm wall and a cold rough tree.
I am all I taste.
I remember the first time I tasted ice cream.
I am all I remember.
I remember having a toy tractor running over the flowers
Pretending to be in a monster truck.
I am all I've been taught.
I remember being taught not to put a bag over my head.
I am all I think.
When I think I think of playing for Man U.
I am like.
I am like a closed door
But one day someone will open it and see what's inside.
I am the unknown man of the future.

William Jones (12)
Llandrindod High School

I AM . . .

I am all I see, children playing, people walking.
The deputy head picking up rubbish,
TV stars in their best outfit on TV
And pupils working in their bases.
I am all I hear, 'Turn that TV off.'
'Get up and wash your face.'
'Do your homework.'
'Go away Rhi.'
I am all I feel, the pen in my hand,
The touch of my friend's hand on my shoulder.
The touch of chewing gum under my table
And the touch of an animal's fleece.
I am all I taste, the cold milk in my cornflakes on my teeth.
The taste of Sunday dinner watering in my mouth.
I am all I remember, a little sweet girl, my first day at school.
I remember my first tooth falling out.
I am all I've been taught, don't smoke, don't take drugs, stay healthy.
ABCs and 123 . . .
I am all I think, a bubbly person, trying to stay friends with everyone
I like.
I am like a little dog, but when I grow up I'll be a lovely beautiful dog
That's playful and helpful.
I am the girl of the world, that is very helpful.

Rhian Hammond (11)
Llandrindod High School

ODE TO TYRON

My best friend he loves to share
We like to talk, just standing there
He makes me laugh till I'm bright red
He likes the smell of my mum's white bread
We're always up to something fun

Until we're caught by my mum
I've known my friend for four whole years
And all that time there's been few tears
He may be the lad with the sticky out ears
But when he's with me, he'll have no fears.

Brock Sandeman (11)
Llandrindod High School

I AM THE GIRL OF THE FUTURE

I am all I see.
I see girls chatting about girly things and
A group of boys all arguing.
I am all I hear.
I hear mothers shouting and people telling secrets.
I am all I feel.
I feel cotton wool going inside myself and
The mushy noises of leaves.
I am all I taste.
The taste of sugary sweets and the sickly taste of cabbage.
I am all I remember.
People saying things and bullies pushing everyone.
I am all I've been taught.
I try to remember what I've been taught
Like hazards and drugs and smoking
That's bad for your health.
I am all I think.
I think of pop stars singing from their heads
And poor people in the street ill and sick.
I am like an angel falling into the sea
But without the wings.
I am the girl of the future.

Jazmine Ruth Stone (11)
Llandrindod High School

I Am . . .

I am all I see,
Boys playing football, girls learning netball.
My kitten playing on the sofa.
I am all I hear,
My mum gossiping on the phone.
Bob the postman singing.
My CD player playing Atomic Kitten.
I am all I feel,
A comfy bed, my soft teddy.
A handwriting pen.
I am all I taste,
Chocolate chip ice cream,
Coca-Cola, a big fry-up for breakfast.
I am all I remember,
My brother being born.
Swimming for the county,
Starting primary school.
I am all I've been taught.
How to walk, talk, read and write.
To respect others.
I am all I think,
What's going to happen in EastEnders.
How many new friends I'm going to make.
I am like a hedgehog rolled up in a ball
But one day I will unroll,
So the future better be ready for me.
I am the future's freedom.

Lynette Wozencraft (12)
Llandrindod High School

I AM...

I am all I see.
Boys fighting,
Girls talking,
Teachers patrolling the playground,
Classrooms empty.
I am all I hear.
Children talking,
Balls smashing against walls,
The stomping of people running past.
I am all I feel.
I can feel the smoothness of the railings
Going down the steps,
The roughness of the concrete,
The slight prickliness of the grass.
I am all I taste.
I can still taste the chicken tikka I had for lunch,
The orange juice dripping down my throat.
I am all I remember.
Going on lots of holidays,
Playing football,
My first day of high school.
I am all I've been taught.
'Say no to drugs and cigarettes.'
Friends and family are important.
I am all I think.
Who is going to win the football?

Chris Simmons (11)
Llandrindod High School

RUGBY

I'm on the ground trying to get up.
Everybody is dog piling on me.
Trying to get up is very difficult.
The ball under me, throw it out to one of my team members
He goes and scores the try.
It was worth it.

I'm on the ground again.
Everybody is jumping on me,
Trying to get the ball.
Someone kicks me on the leg.
A river of red comes from my knee.
I'm bleeding,
The blood rushes faster still.
The medical man comes running on the pitch.
I get carried off the pitch.
The full-time whistle blows.
We have won!
But where was I?
Inside, missing all the fun.

Daniel Thomas Drew (11)
Llandrindod High School

A DREAM FRIEND

My dream is to have a friend
Who's really kind and great,
A friend forever,
To leave me never,
To be my bestest mate.

A friend to keep
Wherever I go,
A friend that I
Would always know.

A friend for me,
A friend like you.
I wish I had one,
Wouldn't you?

Phillip Venter (12)
Llandrindod High School

I AM . . .

I am all I see.
Boys fighting,
Girls slapping,
Teachers talking.
I am all I hear.
People shouting nasty words,
People laughing to and fro,
I am all I feel.
I feel a soft fluffy cushion from head to toe,
I am all I taste,
Sweet and sour chicken
That runs away at the sight of boys.
I am all I remember.
I am an ant
So small and dull,
I am all I've been taught,
I am a naughty little creature that climbs the walls.
I am all I think.
I am a bit intelligent and a bit dull at times.
I am like a fluffy white kitten but
One day I will be a tiger.
I am the lady of the future.

Amy Smith (11)
Llandrindod High School

MAN U

There's Ferdinand, Scholes,
Van Nistlerooy and Beckham.
They're all the best,
Well, that's what I reckon.
They can score,
They can tackle,
They can save,
They can *win!*
They play for Man U,
Oh yes, they do!
There's Ferdinand, Scholes,
Van Nistlerooy and Beckham.
They're all the best,
Well, that's what I reckon.

There's Ferdinand, Scholes,
Van Nistlerooy and Beckham.
They're all the best,
Well, that's what I reckon.
They've got really good hairstyles,
They're just so cool,
I'd love to have one
But I'm a girl.
I love to play football,
It's my favourite hobby.
There's Ferdinand, Scholes,
Van Nistlerooy and Beckham,
They're all the best,
Well, that's what I reckon!

Kay Powell (11)
Llandrindod High School

CHELSEA

Blue is the colour
To wear
With Pride
Chelsea rises above
All others
Zola strikes, he scores . . .
A goal!
And Hasselbaink scores
A hat-trick!
The crowd goes wild!
When they score a goal,
Up on the big screen,
A lion appears!
Chelsea's mascot!
The thrill of seeing my team playing live
Stays with me forever!
When they approach the goal
I hear the seats clicking
As the spectators stand
To watch them shoot.
Will they score?
The thrill travels up my spine.
The horn hoots,
The whistle blows,
The end of the match is coming.
The players run off the pitch
Taking glory with them
And taking victory back to
Stamford Bridge!

Joshua Dunn (11)
Llandrindod High School

DREAMS

I dream about being a famous singer
And having loads of fans,
When I'm at concerts,
Everyone wants my autograph
And shouts my name,
They hold banners up saying 'Beck',
I would feel nervous,
If I was standing on a stage,
In front of loads of people,
I'm dreading what it will be like,
When I walk onto the stage,
I start singing my first song,
Everyone is cheering,
It's called 'Dear Diary',
I am American,
I look like Britney Spears.
When I finish my first song
I start to talk to my audience,
Then I sing another song,
It's called 'Girl In My Mirror'.
Then some dancers come on,
They start dancing
To entertain the audience.
When I get changed for the next song,
I'm wearing a red leather mini skirt,
Red leather boots and a red T-shirt
With a red leather jacket.
Then I come on and start singing my first line,
'Say hello to the girl that I am',
Everyone is singing along and waving their banners,
Now I have been singing for five hours,
It's the end of my concert, exhilarated but tired,
I curl up and go to bed.

Becky Hughson (11)
Llandrindod High School

I Am...

I am all I see!
My sisters fighting, Mum cooking the dinner
Teachers shouting at the pupils,
Pupils eating their nice dinner
Boys playing football on the field
I am all I hear.
People shouting, I hear doors slamming.
Children shouting across the class.
I hear the footsteps of people running.
I am all I feel.
I feel the warm toast and the lovely warm plates,
The smooth tables, my lovely soft pillows.
I am all I taste.
The perfume in the girls' changing room,
The cold milk from the fridge,
The cold cream in the twisters.
I am all I remember.
The teachers shouting,
Eating nice warm chips at lunch.
Me waking up in the nice warm bed,
Sitting in the classroom working hard.
I am all I think.
People whispering about me,
Me getting lost,
I am like a scared little crab
But one day
I'm coming out of my shell!
I am the crab of the future!

Delyth Wozencraft (11)
Llandrindod High School

I AM...

I am all I see.
Boys fighting in the grass,
Mum watching TV all evening.
I am all I hear.
I hear my name called to have my hair washed,
'Come and help me please,' I hear,
Rain tapping on the window.
I am all I feel.
I feel soft grass under my toes.
I am all I taste.
I taste chicken nuggets sizzling in my mouth.
I am all I remember.
When I was sick as a pig on a boat into the sea.
I am all I've been taught.
'Sit down, get your pencil cases out and books out please.'
I am all I think.
I think like an elephant, but I never get anywhere.
I am like a dolphin but I will be born again.
I am the girl of the future.

Sasha Jackaman (11)
Llandrindod High School

HOBBIES

An orange and black
Blur whizzing by
Is it a tiger running by?
With its glaring eyes
And whistling wheels
You'd better run fast because
I'm hot on your heels!

Ben Harman (11)
Llandrindod High School

MY FEAR OF CENTIPEDES

I'm terrified of centipedes
With all their creepy legs.
They really give me the shivers inside
Whenever I see one I want to hide.
I can't bear to be anywhere near one,
They're freaky and they're creepy,
Worse than my little brother.
I don't really understand
How people have them on their hands.
I couldn't do it,
I'd probably scream!

Everyone says they're more scared of me,
I don't believe that.
They crawl really fast
With their hundreds of legs.
They're freaky and they're creepy,
Worse than my little brother.
I'm terrified of centipedes.

Amy Powell (11)
Llandrindod High School

FEARS

Leaning over a really high bridge,
Overlooking all the dirty water and jagged rocks.
What's under the water? Who knows?
A trolley or a car maybe?
Imagine my mates jumping off that,
Will they? Will they survive?
Who knows?

Joanne Davies (11)
Llandrindod High School

I Am...

I am all I see.
My sister playing with my mum in the garden,
My dad reading the newspaper.
The boys and girls fighting in the school playground.
I am all I hear.
The morning and home time bell,
The teachers shouting or giving information to the students,
Then when I go home I hear my sister shouting
When she can't get her own way!
I am all I feel.
The old sticky chewing gum under the school tables and chairs.
At home the soft thick skin of my sister's hands
And my mum putting her big hands around me.
I am all I taste.
The cold Frosties and milk and the hot chips at the school cafe.
The horrible taste of Bertie Bots every flavour beans.
I am all I remember.
Having my first tooth coming through and me with rosy red cheeks.
I remember my first day at the high school,
Feeling nervous, shy and scared.
I am all I've been taught.
'Never smoke, you could get cancer, and never take drugs
from anyone.'
How to walk and ride a bike,
I am all I think.
Playing netball and wanting to win!
Getting a good level in all my work.
I am the little netballer
But when I grow up I'll be a netballer for Wales.
I am like an egg of a hen,
Just waiting to crack.

Rhian Mills (11)
Llandrindod High School

I AM...

I am all I see.
Children running and laughing.
Birds singing bright and early.
People working hard.
Girls making a fuss over their hair and make-up.
I am all I hear.
'Get up and get ready for school.'
'Stop fighting, behave.'
'Be quiet and do your work.'
My sister on the phone to her fiancé for hours.
I am all I feel.
Our soft kitten when he's sleeping.
My dogs' rough tongues when they lick me on the face.
I am all I taste.
Ham and pineapple pizza.
Mint choc chip ice cream.
Fattening but lovely chips.
I am all I remember.
My kitten being born a year ago.
Us having our dogs when they were puppies.
Charlie, our eldest dog, helping us unwrap our presents
                                    at Christmas time.
My sister wrapping me up in tinsel.
I am all I've been taught.
How to write a biography.
How to talk, walk and write.
How to say the alphabet.
I am all I think.
All my secrets deep down inside me.
Everything that's happening in the world.
I am like a bird in an egg,
But one day I will break free.
I am the unknown future.

Deborah Harrison (11)
Llandrindod High School

I Am . . .

I am all I see.
Boys talking, girls walking, my brother playing.
I am all I hear.
'Go out to play, it's a sunny day.'
I am all I feel.
Sharp nails making a tree house,
Rough bark climbing up trees.
I am all I taste.
Mushy peas running down the side
Of a plate of chips.
Red-hot chillies burning your mouth as you spit them out.
I am all I remember.
Playing my first football game,
Making my first tree den for my first time.
I am all I've been taught.
'Never speak to strangers.'
'The vowels are A, E, I, O, U.'
I am all I think.
Ryan Giggs scoring a free kick,
Wales winning the World Cup.
I am like a boxer but one day
I will knock down my opponent.
I am the David Beckham of the future.

Tyrone McFadden (11)
Llandrindod High School

My Sister Laura

When my sister's angry,
She takes it out on me.
When she's in charge,
She won't let me watch TV.
But when I'm upset,
She cheers me up.

When I'm low on money,
She also tops it up.
She buys me things.
Laura's the best sister.
She's always there
When I need her.

Jonathan Kilby Phillips (11)
Llandrindod High School

I AM...

I am all I see.
People playing football, people eating their lunch.
I am all I hear.
'Tidy your bedroom.' 'Stop bullying your brother.'
I am all I feel.
Falling from a stool and fracturing my wrist,
Hamster feet walking up my arm.
I am all I taste.
Skips melting on my tongue.
Chocolate slipping in my mouth.
I am all I remember.
Falling in the playground dislocating my finger.
I am all I've been taught.
Don't smoke, it damages your lungs.
I am all I think.
Just what will happen in the future.
I am like a fly and these things are the web I am stuck in,
But one day someone will save me because
I'm the man of the future.

Stephen Baker (11)
Llandrindod High School

I Am . . .

I am all I see.
I am the tree branches swaying in the wind.
I am all I hear.
I am the sound of the pebbles being crushed under a car tyre.
I am all I feel.
I am the pain that afflicts me when I trip.
I am all I taste.
I am the taste of a sweet sliding down my throat.
I am all I remember.
I am all the voices that I remember from when I was young.
I am all I've been taught.
I before E except after C.
I am the thought of Creed singing in front of thousands of adoring fans.
I am like a . . .
I am like a telly, I've got to do as I am told. When you press a button
On a remote the telly does what you tell it to unless it's broken
And I've got to do as I'm told.
I am the . . .
I am the leaves dropping from a tree.
I am the flowers ready for picking.
I am nature.

Ryan Watson (11)
Llandrindod High School

View Of A Fox

A sly mover
A tiptoe walker
A keen smeller
A chattering caller
A night-time hunter, sharply listening

Ears pricked tall, wide eyes glistening
Proudly prancing, body leaping high
Its red bushy tail brushes the sky
A silent creeper, with an eerie wail,
Gracefully dancing through the vale.

Eirys Brett (11)
Llandrindod High School

I AM THE WOMAN OF THE FUTURE

I am all I see.
Trees blowing in the wind, hills in the distance
All different colours of green.
I am all I hear.
Music loudly playing especially Slipknot when I am at youth club
And my brother shouting all different things.
I am all I feel.
Snow in my shoes all cold, soft grass under my feet.
I am all I taste.
Ice cream melting on my tongue.
I am all I remember.
Going to Oakwood and getting really wet on Hydro.
I am all I've been taught.
'I before E except after C.'
I am all I think.
Secrets deep down inside.
I am like a box trapped together
But one day I will burst open,
Because I am a woman of the future.

Laura Price (11)
Llandrindod High School

NIGHTMARE

We're trapped
My cousin, my sisters and I
In a farm
With lots of people.
We are hiding
From some men,
They are chasing us.
We hide
In a stable
That has a white horse in it.
They walk past,
We run to some bales,
They walk in,
Look around
But don't see us.
My heart is pounding,
They hear a noise,
They look up,
It is me,
I moved.
They waited for a while
Then they go.
I am so scared I clutch hold of my sister
And hide under the bed and cry.
They come in
And I wake every night.

Hayley Smith (11)
Llandrindod High School

FAMILY

I have a brother called Richard.
He's 13 and a bully.
He hits me,
Kicks me,
Punches me in the tummy.
He's never any fun,
Just like a broken drum
Richard is boring.

I have a nine-year-old sister called Laura.
She's piano crazy.
When I'm watching telly,
She plays away very heavily.
I shout, 'Oh please shut up,'
But she doesn't listen,
She just carries on.
Laura is so annoying.

I have a sister called Sarah.
She's six and she's the worst of the lot.
She gets my things out and
Never puts them back.
Sometimes she even breaks them.
When we're both in the lounge
She shouts, 'Mum, Mum! James just hit me.'
Grrrr!

James Powell (12)
Llandrindod High School

FLYING

Oh, how I wish I could fly,
Just by spreading my arms out wide
And think where I'm going.
Oh, how good it would be to fly,
I could see the towns and cities 200 feet above Earth
And laugh and point at people who are as small as ants.
Oh, how magical it would be to fly,
I could fly along with birds migrating south.
Oh, how it would be great to fly.
I could circle the planets, float around with the asteroids
And see our solar system's many mysteries.
Oh, how magnificent it would be to fly,
I could see another universe that no one else -
Not even a scientist could see.
Oh, it would be good to have a dream come true.

Kyle William David Watson (12)
Llandrindod High School

MY FAMILY

My dad is called Colin you see
And he's the head of our family.
My mum Janet is busy all day
And keeps us happy in work and play.
Brother Barry is home on the farm
And keeps very calm.
Brother Alun is after the girls
And has lots of curls.
I'm the next in the family,
Always smiling and happy.
Sister Bronwen loves to dance
If she has a chance.

Anwen Evans (13)
Llandrindod High School

I AM...

I am all I see, the football on the TV.
My mum when I get home
And the hills and mountains in the distance.
I am all I hear, the trees rustling in the wind
And the sound of cars rushing by.
I am all I feel, the first time I touched the salty water of the sea.
I am all I taste, the sour taste of fizzy sweets
And the sweet taste of Coke.
I am all I remember, my first day of high school.
I am all I've been taught, my times tables and how to spell.
I am all I think, scoring the winning goal of the World Cup.
I am like an ice cube but one day I'll melt.
I am the man of the future.

Toby Hay (11)
Llandrindod High School

I AM...

I am all I see, I see the whiteboard being written on
And people getting rammed into the door, day after day.
I am all I hear, I hear rubbish rattling across the empty playground.
I am all I feel, I feel a chair being sat on by a ton of bricks.
I am all I taste, I taste a turkey burger because of its sweetness.
I am all I remember, I remember calling my sister 'fishfingers'.
I am all I've been taught, I've been taught to round my letters off.
I am all I think, I think of GCSEs and SATs in Year 9.
I am like a piece of rubbish but in a good way.
I am the thing of the future.

Jamie Venables (11)
Llandrindod High School

I AM THE SUPER GIRL OF THE FUTURE

I am all I see.
The bright colours swirling around me,
My friends having fun and people being joyful.
I am all I hear.
People nattering, 'Hurry up.' 'Come on.'
My dog howling, crash, whispering like the wind blowing.
I am all I feel.
Ice cream melting down my throat,
My cushy smooth bed,
Me melting into the sofa.
I am all I taste.
Cornflakes crunching in my mouth,
The sour taste of salt on my tongue.
I am all I remember.
Mathematical sums whizzing round my head,
The clock ticking in my ear as time goes by,
My brother nagging me to shut up.
I am all I've been taught.
'Don't talk to strangers.' 'Be careful.'
'Don't do this.' 'Don't do that.'
English, RE, PE, Welsh, geography, history, science.
I am all I think.
Daydreaming about colours, wonders,
What's going to happen next,
Teachers telling me to do something.
I am like.
A monkey climbing up trees,
Like a butterfly, always jolly
And looking for some fun.
But sometimes like a deer
Quite sad and lonely,
Not knowing what's going to happen next,
I am the super girl of the future.

Rhiannon Holdaway (11)
Llandrindod High School

I AM...

I am all I see.
People running because the bell's just gone!
Horses cantering round the long meadows playing in the breeze.
I am all I hear:
My baby brother crying for his milk!
'Come on play with him, he's only a baby.'
I am all I feel:
Ouch, I forgot how to ice skate. I fell on my bum!
Oh god, I'd fallen out of the saddle and was clinging on for my life
Round poor Splash's neck.
I was tacking my horse Penny up and she trod on my foot.
Her hoof is bigger than an orange. Mine was too after that!
I am all that I taste:
Chocolate melting in my mouth.
Crisps going crunch as I eat them.
I am all that I remember:
Sadness leaving primary school.
Excited about high school at the same time.
I am all I've been taught:
'Be good, don't shout, write neat, sit tall, don't drool.'
I am all that I think:
Hey I better sit tight on a roller coaster going down the steepest of hills.
I am like all those things,
But I walk away
Because I'm the woman of the future.

Lucy Bevan (11)
Llandrindod High School

MY BROTHERS

I don't like my brothers, they ruin everything.
They mess up my room. Everything is then a tip.
They jump on my bunk and throw my books around.
I don't know what I've done to them.
Oh no, here they come,
I wish I had a lock on the door.
They're annoying, they're nasty, they'll wait till I move from the door.
Oh no! They're in and my room is a mess again.
At least they won't bother me outside.
I'll ride my bike around the house.
I'm riding, so far so good, I hope they don't see me.
Oh no, they're on their bikes.
They've got water pistols, I must get off, I don't want to get wet,
I don't know where my brother is.
He must have gotten fed up.
There he is, he's riding the other way
And behind me is my other brother.
'I'm trapped,' they always win.

Lewis Smith (11)
Llandrindod High School

HOBBIES

Being on my quad bike
Is my favourite thing to do
As blue as the colour of sky
The quad travels as fast as the waves.
When I'm going fast it's not scary at all.
But when I'm in a race,
It is scary, but it's cool!

I'm finally in the lead,
One more lap to go.
Faster, faster until I finish the race!
I'm so cool!
I stand on top of the stage,
Very, very nervous.
But at the same time proud as I lift that cup of mine.

Declan Austin (11)
Llandrindod High School

MY PETS

I think my pets are quite adventurous
they get to the strangest places.
My crocodile escaped down the loo
my hamster escaped through the cat flap
and my parrot is in my cap.
My dog chased a van to Australia
but my cat died . . . it sniffed my dad's shoe
and went *phew!* and collapsed onto the floor.
My rabbit had bunnies, about 176 in all.
One day she had a few more and sat on the floor
just as the hutch gave way.
My goldfish got into the washing machine
and when he came out to no surprise, he was squeaky clean.
My frog went out with the dirty water
but fortunately my sister caught her
then it started to rain, oh what a pain
so she dropped it down the drain.

Chris Morgan (11)
Llandrindod High School

SPIDERS

I screamed, I was running,
Dreaming.
Spiders, no smaller than the awful terror.
What shall I do?
Down the gutter, all slimy,
The awful terror pinned me to the floor.
The big fangs, gooey, with spit!
What shall I do?
The long, hairy leg touching me.
Chills run down my spine.
The scary, big, brown body looked like chocolate.
I wish it was, I could gobble it down whole.
I scream, I wake, I realise there was no spider in front of me but . . .
I look under the bed
To make sure, just in case.

Darrilyn Ruell (11)
Llandrindod High School

MY PET

My pet is lovely,
He sleeps all night,
He slithers up trees,
He's very disguisable.
He's green with a long tail,
His tongue is long,
He pokes it out
And makes rude signs at me.
His skin is rough
And bumpy to the touch.
His name is Draco,
Can you guess what he is yet?

Jade Davis (11)
Llandrindod High School

SNAKES

Snakes are slimy and scaly,
They make me shiver inside,
If I ever saw one I would run a mile outside
All they do is slither through the long green grass,
Eating everything that just happens to run past,
If I ever had one on my neck,
I would let out a scream, 'Bloomin' 'eck!'
Their eyes are like diamonds,
Shining in the sun,
Their tongue is like a train,
It is always on the run,
Always eating and chewing,
Till the set of the sun.

Laura Hughes (11)
Llandrindod High School

I LOVE FRIENDS

Friends are cool,
Friends are funky,
They make me laugh and giggle.
Wherever we are we make trouble.
Whenever I'm on my own I feel rather alone.
We love having fun
Especially in the sun.

Life is good with friends,
I never want it to end.
Sometimes they drive me around the bend,
But we mend it in the end.
I love friends!

Laura Jones (12)
Llandrindod High School

Fox Hunting

People can be so cruel,
Picking on animals
Who have never done anything to them
And probably never will.

Animals can't fight back,
They can't defend themselves,
They're no match for us
With our weapons and our guns.

Take fox hunting for instance,
How can people be so cruel?
They treat it as a sport,
Chasing foxes and ripping them to shreds.

I mean, how would you feel
Being chased by hounds,
Getting breathless from running,
Knowing you'll have to give up?

But you can't
Cos then they'll get you
And who knows what they'll do?
You have to keep running.

You hide behind a tree,
The dogs stop and look round,
They put their noses to the ground,
Sniffing for your scent.

They come closer and closer,
You know you don't have much time,
Their noses pressed to the floor,
They're closing in!

The circle's getting tighter,
Soon there'll be nowhere out . . .

Silence,
Peace at last.

Rebecca Davies (11)
Llandrindod High School

FEARS

I have a fear and produce a tear,
Whenever I see a spider
They glide on their webs
From the ceiling.
Their big black coats
Aren't as coarse as goats,
But I still have a fear of spiders.

When I go to bed
I think in my head
That there's one in the corner of my room,
I am so scared
I cannot sleep,
I look at the moon instead.

When I see one
I freeze in one spot,
Their hairy legs
Make me shiver,
I run down the stairs
And tell my mum,
Then she moves it
Which makes me feel better.

Sian Acton (11)
Llandrindod High School

I AM...

I am all I see.
My friends playing about.
My brother munching sweets.
My family laughing happily.
I am all I hear.
My brother playing his guitar at top whack.
'Go have a shower, now!'
'Get out of my room.'
I am all I feel.
My brother and I having a scrap.
Going for an adventure in the puddles and mud.
Brambles scratching my body.
I am all I taste.
The taste of freshly picked fruit.
My mum's super tasting cakes.
Sweets fizzing on my tongue.
I am all I remember.
I remember jumping on my dad.
Getting my very first pet.
Having fun with my dog.
I am all I've been taught.
'Never fight.'
'Don't smoke!'
'Don't get dirty, or you're for it.'
I am all I think.
Deep emotions.
Secrets.
I am like a Father Bear
And these are my things,
But one day they will move on
And be free, because
I am the man of the future.

Christopher Thomas (11)
Llandrindod High School

HOBBIES

My hobby is playing football,
I can beat my dad.
I dribble around him and score a goal.
I love taking free kicks and corners
And even penalties.
I kick as fast as a cheetah
And run like a motorbike.
I dive like I'm going down a slide.
When I play, the sweat trickles
Down my face - my face gets hot.
I'm just about to burst and then the ball
Comes flying in like a golden eagle.
The top of my foot makes contact with the ball
And it goes in the goal
Like Concorde going a million miles an hour.
I celebrate, like it's my birthday.
90 minutes pass, there is three minutes' stoppage time.
What a relief, because there is more time to score,
But then the opposition scores. *Panic.*
I pray that I can score. I keep hitting the post,
Sweat trickles down my face even more
And it is a corner, and they score again
And then I'm really mad.
I do my best to score one more.

Daniel Summers (11)
Llandrindod High School

MY HOBBY

Airfix is my hobby,
I really like it lots,
I think it's a lovely activity,
Whether it's raining or whether it's shining
Airfix is my hobby.

In the sunny summer months
I do it at a table,
Outside it dries so fast it's unbelievable.

In the ice-cold winter months
I do it inside in the warm,
I listen to tapes for company,
The only problem is
I have to leave the models to dry.

Carefully I cut the pieces off the sprue,
I file them down until they're smooth,
Then accurately I apply the glue
And firmly press the pieces together.

After I've built the model
I paint it precisely,
Then with water, I apply the transfers.
After such painstaking work,
Voila,
My piece of art.

Mark Davies (11)
Llandrindod High School

MY TEACHER

My teacher is a pain, she is,
She drives me up the wall,
She thinks she's very cool you know,
But she's not that cool at all!

She wears all these hippie clothes
And has no taste at all,
She wears these trousers too big for her
And shoes as big as Mars!

When we entered a competition
For the best story,
I didn't win at all,
But I don't care
I'll try again next year!

Last year when it was Hallowe'en
She gave us all a fright,
She climbed upon a window sill
And shouted, 'Get out or else I'll bite!'
There was us running down the road,
Hiding from the beast,
But all it was, was Mrs Beach
Shouting to children,
Only asking for sweets.

That is why my teacher is a pain!

Holly Collard (12)
Llandrindod High School

MY SISTER'S ROOM

I am terrified of my sister's room
The glowing pink all around me
Then I turn around and straight in front of me is an S Club 7 CD
And then, there, on her bed, a Winnie the Pooh book
And on her cabinet a pink fluffy lampshade.
Arghh!
My skin starts to shiver.
I am terrified,
Pink fluff
Urghh!
And then she comes in.
'Do you want a kissy wissy?'
No!
I run under the bed and hide for my life.
I smell her disgusting socks. I cannot breathe
Then she sees me. I run
I survive!

Daniel Gough (11)
Llandrindod High School

FRIENDS

There're lots of friends that I've lost and found,
When we are together we make a dreadful sound.
Everywhere we go we have some fun,
Underneath the big red sun.
We eat, drink and play together,
I hope that we are friends forever.

Amy Lewis (11)
Llandrindod High School

WHO'S OUT THERE?

Late at night, it's turned twelve o'clock,
Your next-door neighbour gets ready to *pounce,*
Everyone's asleep except your next-door neighbour.
No one's outside, not even your cat,
Do not let this scare you, she might be back tonight.

With her black cat and her broom,
Don't go near South Street,
There's a house, not any old house,
The House of Doom!

Keep away from that house.

There's a witch in there,
A witch in disguise!

Jayne L Shepherd (11)
Llandrindod High School

DREAMS

Monday night you dream about monsters,
Tuesday night you talk to yourself in your sleep,
Wednesday night you dream about getting wed,
Thursday night you dream about being a tree,
Friday night you have a freaky dream,
Saturday night you sing in your dream,
Sunday night you have a scary dream,
If you mix them all together, you would have a weird dream.

Leila Tribe (11)
Llandrindod High School

SCARY SPIDERS

Spiders are black,
They sometimes hide in a potato sack.
Long, hairy legs
That scuttle along the floor!
I have nothing to do but scream
As they come towards me with a huge team!

Examine a spider up close
You'll be shocked at the fangs
Ready for a kill.
People tell me to chill.
What happens when they grow 8ft tall?
I know the human population will fall!
Will I be alright, when the spiders
Go in for the bite?
Spiders are scary
Full stop!

Rosie Knight (11)
Llandrindod High School

MY BROTHER

I have a brother,
His name is Jack
And he is a bully and that is that.
He is stronger than me so he takes advantage
But on the odd occasion he is alright,
Like when he lets me watch TV,
But when he takes it too far
I wish I could get revenge,
But when I try
I come away with a bruise or two.

Samuel Williams (11)
Llandrindod High School

MY BROTHER

Brothers can be so annoying,
Crying for no reason,
Getting me into trouble,
Sometimes he can be . . .
Pleasant (only sometimes though).
When he is pleasant
He gives me pleasurable things,
Ice creams, sweets and . . .
Oh the list goes on.
Brothers are nice to have,
I can play football with him,
I can use him to get people into trouble,
Get me lovely stuff, like food and lovely treats.
Sometimes he is willing to do
Anything for me.

Naomi Sullivan (11)
Llandrindod High School

MY DREAMS

I'd like to meet David Beckham
And play in the World Cup.
I play for England and Man U,
I'd earn a lot of money
And be a millionaire,
Own a limo,
Drive around,
Own a speedboat,
Go abroad,
Be famous
And have a big family
And have a happy life.

David Ramplee (11)
Llandrindod High School

SUPER MUM

My mum is like a grizzly bear
With all that curly facial hair,
I don't know what to do,
Some say my mum's a super human? I don't think it's true,
I think she's kind of weird
With that greying curly beard,
I think she is from space,
Or some stupid unknown place,
She cleans the house from bottom to top
Flying on her super mop,
My mum is rather mad
And she looks a little sad,
When I cheer her up and say, 'It's alright,'
Her eyes begin to glow so bright,
My mum's a super human! Now I know it's true,
People come from near and far to see what she can do.

Shane Healey (13)
Llandrindod High School

FEAR

I'm afraid of death,
Honest I'm not dying,
I curl up and start crying
When I think of people dying.

I'm afraid of dying,
Of having a never-ending spell,
In a coffin all alone,
Turning into dust and bone.

Death is such an awful word,
Everyone just hates it.
After all it is quite scary.
Tuberculosis, cancer, accidents they all can kill,
Hey watch out it could come here for you.

Liam Robinson (11)
Llandrindod High School

GONE FISHIN'

Splash the dead mackerel falls into the blue sea,
I quickly reel it in through the water.
Then wham!
A huge yellow fin tuna takes the bait,
Whizz!
The line starts to fly off the spool,
I reel and reel!
The sweat is running down my face,
The rod is bending,
Then suddenly I see the shape
Getting bigger and bigger.
The fish has one last tug on the line,
I grab the net!
I lift it out of the water onto the scales,
The needle flies around to 68lb,
The fish kicks and I lift it up and drop it into the water,
I steer the boat home with a big, wide smile.

Ben Griffiths (11)
Llandrindod High School

AMERICAN FOOTBALL

American football is fun,
When I play my knees shake.
I run like lightning,
I have a ball tucked under my arm.
I am small but I am quick,
I run away before the kick.
When my opponents run towards me
They look like big, huge bears
Who are indestructible.
The whistle goes, my hearts starts to beat,
I can feel the thundering of their feet.
When I go to catch the ball
I wonder if I'm going to fall.
When I catch the ball in my vision
I see these bears, scarier than nuclear fission.

Karl Harris (11)
Llandrindod High School

MY PET

Chunky and hunky is my pet,
Big floppy ears
And a nose that's wet.
Feet the size of large breeze blocks,
Teeth the size of lollipops.
He's fat and lazy
With a tail that's wavy.
With not much to do
He'd be dead excited to see you.

Aaron Martin (11)
Llandrindod High School

DOWN HILLING

When the gate drops
That's when I paddle off
Down the track
Without looking back,
Dodging in and out of trees,
Sliding on the fallen leaves.
Spinning the back wheel round and round
I fall with a thud and hit the ground.
With a bent and battered bike and a hurting shin
I jump back on the broken thing
And speed on down the bumpy track,
Trying not to hurt my back.
When the finish line's in sight
I jump the jump and I'm in flight.
When I cross the chequered line
That's when I know that glory's mine.

Matthew Baynham (13)
Llandrindod High School

MY DAD

My dad says I'm stupid,
My dad says I'm thick,
My dad says I'm a little brat who likes to spit,
My dad says I'm ignorant,
My dad says that I'm rude
But then my dad laughs at himself
And says I'm just like him too.

Sarah Woodward (12)
Llandrindod High School

MY BROTHER

My brother is annoying, he hits me every day,
He's even got me with a baseball bat,
He said that I would pay!
Next he threw a stone, it just missed my head,
Then I ran after him and locked him in my shed.
On my birthday my friend came round to play,
My brother threw water bombs at us, we were soaking wet all day.
On Christmas Day he said he'd gotten me a present,
He told me to look in my bed, so I ran upstairs to find
A great big spider.
I ran after him shouting he was going to be dead.
That's why he is annoying, he hits me every day,
One day I'm going to get him and send him far away,
Hopefully he won't come back and hit me every day.

Nathan Davies (12)
Llandrindod High School

MY FAMILY

My family is special to me,
They're sweet and stingy like a honeybee.
My dad is Welsh and proud.
My grandad's head is in the cloud.
My mum is small and blonde,
Sometimes I think she'd like to abscond.
My dog is sweet and sound,
He chases his tail round and around.
My sister is about to become a mummy
And if you see her she has a big tummy.
My family is special to me,
They're sweet and stingy like a honeybee.

Rachel Williams (13)
Llandrindod High School

MY FAMILY

My family is really noisy and a pain,
They nick my stuff and drive me insane.
I have three sisters,
Ceri, Elin and Delyth.
Ceri is always angry and mad at whatever I do,
I sometimes wonder if she has a clue.
Elin is always running, everywhere she goes she has to run
And thinks it's really fun.
Delyth is small and spoilt,
She always eats sweets and watches TV.
I don't know why my family are like this
But with them, life is bliss.

Gwenda Wozencraft (12)
Llandrindod High School

FRIENDS

I have two best friends,
They make me laugh.
We all hang out together -
In any kind of weather!
When we go up town
We act like a couple of clowns.
Even sometimes when we row
We seem to fix it somehow.
At the end of the day
I have to say,
Friends are the best -
But sometimes . . .
We all need a rest.

Lauren Morgan (12)
Llandrindod High School

MY BROTHER AND I

Me and my brother don't get on well,
I don't know what he is, I could never tell.
Even though he thinks he's cool
He was even worse when we were in the same school.

OK, maybe we're not that bad
As I try and help him if he's sad.
We kind of like each other sometimes,
Although we can do good impressions of each other's mimes.

The worst thing we've ever done
Is destroy the kitchen in a mad fight,
Although it was kind of good fun
He still threw tea all down me, then made his flight.

We might have done worse than that
But there're too many things, I'll go on for so long.
Once I got him so mad he kicked next door's cat
And that was the end of that.

Heidi Harries (12)
Llandrindod High School

FAMILY

My dad acts like a gorilla
Across the living room floor.
He thumps his chest
And puts on a vest
While he's dancing, next to the door.

My mum is totally different,
She's really, really nice.
She puts credit on my phone
Nearly every day and night.

My sister is so noisy
But she's really, really boring.
Her name is Evie Doman
And she always is performing.

My grandma lives next door to me,
She's really, really sweet.
I go and see her every day
And she sometimes gives me a treat.

Kirsty Doman (11)
Llandrindod High School

MY DOG

My dog is nice and soft
But I don't like him when he bites.
It's annoying when you have to take him for a walk
When you're having a rest.
He stands in front of the TV when you're watching it.
He's mad 'cause he barks at his own face in a mirror.

He chases the cat round the garden
But the cat cuts him with her claws,
So in the end the cat wins!

When the cat sleeps in his bed
The dog gets annoyed,
The dogs falls asleep standing up.
He runs around the garden with a bouncy ball.
I throw it in the air but he forgets where it lands,
He is a stupid dog after all.

Sophie Williams (12)
Llandrindod High School

MY ROOM

My room is so messed up
I can't find anything,
I've lost so many socks,
My mum pays me to clean it,
But I never do it.

If my mountain of dirty clothes
Gets any higher
I'd better buy a tumble dryer.

My Scalextric track
Goes right around the house
And my sister's pet mouse
Goes round and round on it.

I have to admit
My room is a very big tip,
But I like it as it is.

Adam Stephens (13)
Llandrindod High School

MY LITTLE SISTERS

Two weeks premature,
Crawling about on the floor,
They're too loud, we can't get any peace!
Sioned's wearing her little pink fleece,
Sometimes they draw on the walls, Mum goes insane.
Then Lorna says, 'It's only a little plane.'
When it comes to bedtime they really are quite cute,
I'd play them a song if I had a flute.

Thomas Simmons (13)
Llandrindod High School

SAND

I hate sand,
It gets between your toes
And even up your nose.
It gets you by surprise
When it goes in your eyes.
When I went down south
I got it in my mouth.
It feels all gritty,
When you see it, it's all bitty.
It makes me cringe
And gives me a springe.
When it goes in my sandwich
It tastes like garbage.
I hate sand.

Kyle King (12)
Llandrindod High School

MY ROOM

My room is a cool place
Even though it's messy.
It's somewhere I can relax
From the racket downstairs.
It's somewhere I can forget
Everything around me.
In my room I can do what I like,
When I like.
I can listen to music, watch telly!
I can do what I want in my room!

Danielle Cosgrave (13)
Llandrindod High School

FISHING

Fishing is my true hobby.
I like it so very much.
I swing the line out, something chomps at my worm.
Do I strike or do I not?
I strike!
He's on the line!
Do I play him or do I get it over with?
I play the fish.
There it is, splashing in pain.
The rod bends, I say to my dad, 'Get the net.'
Sweat is pouring down my face.
'How much longer?' I say!
At last I see the fish! Is it a carp, a chub, or maybe a pike?
And then it jumps up,
'It's a big one,' I say.
'Have you got that net yet Dad?'
Finally, I land her.
I show my mum, she faints.
I put it on the weighing scales. '30lbs.'
My mum faints again.
We take a photo and look at the fish for a minute or two.
With its slimy body and layers upon layers of shark-like teeth.
Finally we put her back.
She swims away as slow as a tortoise and as stiff as a snail.

Russell Thomas (11)
Llandrindod High School

DREAMS

You can dream awake or asleep,
If the dream's bad let's hope it's not too deep.
Some people dream of different things,
They dream about having wings,
They fly over hills and streams.

While they fly they eat ice creams
So they fly free.
Enjoy your dreams because they're a door
To a land you've never been before.

Vikki Young (13)
Llandrindod High School

YUM - DONUTS

Yum - donuts!
Soft, chewy, sometimes jammy inside,
Sometimes chocolate coated with sprinkles on top.

Yum - donuts!
Once I take a bite out of the donut
A jammy surprise awaits,
Licking the jam off my lips
Is my favourite bit.

Yum - donuts!
Lining up in the queue
Being pushed about
But I don't care, I want my donut!

Yum - donut!
A sugary look and a soft feel,
But don't squeeze too hard
Or the jam will fall out the side
And run down your hands.

Yum - donut!
There's all kinds of donuts,
Dinky Donuts, chocolate donuts,
Plain donuts, too many to mention.

Stuart Eyre (11)
Llandrindod High School

STAN THE SPACEMAN

I once saw a spaceman
Floating round in space
With a bag on his back
And a smile on his face.

He was floating around like Superman
I asked him his name
He said it was 'Stan'
'Stan the spaceman'.

He had black hair
And blue eyes
He was short and fat
And he told lies.

His eyes were like the sea
They shone in the light.
His hair was like coal
As black as the night.

If you look up to the sky tonight
I'm sure you will see an amazing sight
Stan the spaceman
In all his glory and his might.

Nerys Hammond (12)
Llandrindod High School

MY DOG

When I take him for a walk
He'll never stop to let me talk,
He runs on and sees a foe
And then he's off, 'No, no, no!'

He starts a fight and barks and barks
All day until it's dark,
When finally I pull him away
He starts whining so I say,
'We're going home.'

Hannah Lloyd (12)
Llandrindod High School

FAMILY

My dad is Welsh
My mum is Scottish
My dad eats leeks
My mum eats haggis
My brother is a brat
And acts like a prat
My dad's a builder
My mum's a baker
My dad gets drunk
My mum washes up
My brother watches TV.

Me? I am normal
I don't do any wrong.
My mum nags me,
But I make an excuse to go for a pee
Then I go out to call for mates.
When I come in I get something to eat
I go upstairs to wash and brush my teeth
Then I go straight to bed.
Me? I am normal.

David Pritchard (14)
Llandrindod High School

ONE WEIRD DAY

I like nightmares, they are full of blood and guts,
Adrenaline pumping through my veins
Like a murderer hunting their victim,
Running down an everlasting hallway with blood crawling
                                        down the wall,
Heartbeat down to normal rate,
I woke from my sleep and go downstairs.
While eating breakfast I hear my dad say,
'I am the king of this house.'
And I said, 'King of the house, you couldn't be king of a toilet.'
I leave the room and I hear my mum say,
'You haven't finished your breakfast
And you ain't going out of the house
Until you have tidied your room.'
Mum gives me the duster.
Sorry won't be coming out for some time.

Ieuan Hughes (13)
Llandrindod High School

MY BROTHER

My brother is annoying,
as messy as can be
he sits so long on the toilet,
he could miss half of World War III

He's dirty, hyperactive,
he always tells tales to my mom,
you'd think how many biscuits he eats
a catastrophic bomb!

He eats unhygenically,
while parked in front of the TV,
a regular TV addict
always watching channel 3.

My brother is annoying,
as messy as can be,
and I'm always telling him,
'Don't try and bother me!'

Owen Major (12)
Llandrindod High School

MY DAD

My dad is the coolest,
but he is a bit dumb,
he embarrasses me a lot,
in front of all my friends.

One Hallowe'en he dressed up as a witch
he waited for us in a ditch.

On our holidays in sunny France,
he decided to show-off his Oak Valley pants
by dancing round like Michael Flatley
and his dance was very catchy.

There is so much more that I could say,
about him being embarrassing,
and there's a lot of stuff that I could
say about him being a caring father.

But hey, where's the fun in that!

Chloe Davis (12)
Llandrindod High School

MY DOG

My dog is different,
She snores like a man,
She snorts like a pig,
Everyone says
Her face is so scary,
She doesn't bite,
She is really very nice,
She is very small,
She is about the size of a rugby ball,
She skids across the kitchen floor
And runs into the front room door,
My dull brother pulled her by her tail
So she bit him on the fingernail.

Emma Davies (13)
Llandrindod High School

DREAMS

The dream I have at least once a year
Is where I'm sitting in a car.
We're being chased, I don't know why.
The door flies open suddenly.
I hold onto the door with all my strength,
But then as I fall out the car, I wake
And hit my head on my bedroom floor.

Sam Glenton (13)
Llandrindod High School

MY FEARS

My greatest fears are
Spiders with big furry legs
And backs like a hedgehog curled up.
Sharks deep down in the ocean,
Watching and waiting to attack
20 foot crocodiles crawling,
In and out of bushes,
Hiding behind the long, high rushes.
Bears in the outback,
Hunting for food.
But most of all,
The head of English,
In a mood.

Craig Rees (13)
Llandrindod High School

MUM

My mum is the best
But can be a right old pest.
She nags and nags for a cup of tea
And normally she nags me.
Still I love her loads
To me she's made of gold.
When I'm in a mood
She always cheers me up.
She washes my clothes
She cooks my dinner
What else could you want
My mum is a winner!

Alyson Eyval (13)
Llandrindod High School

THE NOT SO GREAT SCHOOL

Some people say school is such a boring place,
for others it puts a smile on their face
people think of it in different ways
but this is what my English teacher says,

'If you don't like it, get used to it
if you do then that's great, isn't it?'

School can be easy, it can be hard
one day you're happy, the next you're sad
there are tests, they stress you out
but this is what my art teacher thinks without a doubt

OK, so tests drive you round the bend
but remember it will be worth it in the end.

We do maths, science and history
we also do art, French and geography
you get detentions for being mean
and this is what any of my teachers do if you get seen.

They will keep you in and make you write lines
and before you start they say, 'Do it 100 times!'

OK, so they are not that bad
and in a way I'm rather glad
but how would I know? I've never been caught.

Oops! I spilled the beans
(umm, in food technology).

Rogrigo Buanafina (12)
Penglais Comprehensive School

YOU

I am who I am and no one can change that,
I can only be myself.
I could dress up as someone but I'd still be me,
You can only be yourself.

You could be an identical twin and swap places,
But you would know who you were.
You could have the eyes of your mum or dad but you're still you,
Because you are unique.

If I was you for a day and you were me,
Then you would see that we are both completely different;
You should not have to be the same as anyone,
It is better to be an individual.

You can never change who you are,
You are who you are and nobody else.
I am who I am and no one can ever change that
I can only be myself.

Helen Welsh (12)
Penglais Comprehensive School

MY LIFE, MY WORLD

The hold the world in a grain of sand
to walk within this wondrous land
to hold your life in your hands
to walk your path untamed and unplanned
I walk my world, from yours I'm banned!

Steven Moss (15)
Penglais Comprehensive School

PEOPLE

When I see crowds of people
I wonder what they're like.
Are they poor and hungry,
Or rich with trainers by Nike?

Are they cruel and evil
And never give a thought
To those with a life of suffering
And animals killed in blood sport?

I wonder if they are foreign,
Or are they related to me?
Are they Jews or Muslims?
I wonder what could be.

Finally, are they nice and kind
Who help at charity too?
But the big question is about to come . . .
Which one of these are *you?*

Ben Williams (12)
Penglais Comprehensive School

THE KARUBELA

Beware of the karubela my son, for he is mad,
For he is furious with me, for killing his conumfress dad,
But if you dare, to go outside,
Take my vorpal sword and use it with pride.

Beware my son, of the monster that slayed,
For his spirit is crazed,
But try my son, try to kill,
Try to kill that horrid thing!

His neck is bobus, his head is huge,
His feet are slithery and his back is muge!
But don't be afraid my son,
For his killing is going to commence!

Then one day, the child was bored,
So he drew his vorpal sword,
He slithered and singed
And death was upon the karubela!

William Hamilton (13)
St Michael's School, Llanelli

POISON

The man got out of his bed
He saw the moneybox open
He looked inside it, everything was gone
He called the police but they didn't do anything.

So he took his own action
He put extra locks on the doors
The next night he went to sleep
He woke up in the morning
To find all his silver gone,
He was angry.

So he put special poison on his valuables
Which if touched without gloves
It will go through the skin and poison the blood.
Leading to a slow painful death.

Night came, he went to bed
And in the morning he was found dead!

Peter Temple (13)
St Michael's School, Llanelli

HE WHO KILLS

They were here before you
Living another day
Died for one another
Slayed and slaughtered for pay

He who kills has no right
Equality means the same
Even though different looks
Nobody's to blame

Killed and murdered for their blood
Death awaits to seize
With no warning one quick blow
Death to them, is disease

It may strike you, with hollow fear
Although you already know
Nobody, really cares
Least of all, one whose feelings are hollow

Money is evil, there are other ways
It is the result of death,
Too late to stop playing the game
Too late to catch a breath

Too late to say goodbye
Not even one last glance
Don't know where they're going
Led in as if in a trance

They can't stop it
They rely on you
So if you, are one who kills
Reverse the situation
Death would soon await you.

Rachel Williams (13)
St Michael's School, Llanelli

THE EXCONEL

Be careful my boy,
Though you shall not fail,
You lurverig, chuning
It will be down in a quail.

Watch out for the Exconel my son,
Thone long sharp horns, and claws of steel.
Also look out for the Werdena
And the deadly Gahana-weel.

The boy tool his sincal axe in hand,
As he prepare for the battle woe,
His axe mank sharp
To slay the foe.

So out he went,
To battle nigh,
His weapon ganned,
His head held high.

Then there it was,
The Exconel zie,
With long horns
And terrifying myie.

He took a suclipe,
But it not mouned back
And with throne claws,
It got him rack.

His head fell off,
And he was no more
The Exconel victorious
And powerful once more.

Jonathan Evans (13)
St Michael's School, Llanelli

WALDO THE WELSH WONDER

This is a tale that is so often told,
Heard and enjoyed by both young and old,
It tells of a creature who is loyal and kind,
A friend who appears, yes, in everyone's mind!

Waldo is there when at times we are sad,
Cheering, encouraging and making us glad,
Whenever we feel moments of terror and fear,
This friendly Welsh wonder always comes near

Sometimes he's angry and makes us feel sorry,
When to other people caused heartache and worry,
A nasty word, an unworthy deed, a little white lie,
Make Waldo a failure, unhappy and cry.

Pray, what can I do? Oh! What can I do?
To help complex beings I haven't got a clue,
They're all so ungrateful, and never content,
Is there an answer to this creature's lament?

No! I will not give up, I've a good job to do,
An honour to be chosen, so I will see it through,
Success will be achieved as you will surely see,
Come on Waldo, get to work, and surprise even me!

Waldo worked hard both by day and by night,
Winning our hearts and showing us what's right,
I believe in him, each day he's always there,
A friendly, helpful creature, I know I'm in his care.

Waldo the Welsh wonder can be your best friend too,
A comfort when in trouble or when you're feeling blue,
Put all your faith in him, listen when he talks to you,
Waldo the Welsh wonder, close by each day anew.

Aled Mathias (13)
St Michael's School, Llanelli

The Tarot Reader

The end of the street, he claimed his place
By the lamp post on the corner
And he put on a smiling face,
His first customer: a mourner.

The cards were picked, a pleasing sight
The Devil, Death and the star were drawn
'I know you've suffered, but delight, for
At the end of the tunnel's a light!'

He carried on till nine o'clock
Then put away his tarot set,
In his wooden box with the lock
And went back home to bed.

That night, the moon was full and bright
The occult magic took its place
Then the man awoke at midnight
And he possessed a startled face

His psychic powers awoke that night
And then he leapt up like the fighter.
Psychokinetic powers and telepathy
Remote viewing and empathy
Overwhelmed him all that night
He then gave up the fight . . .

The morning after, the street was lined
With the trail of destruction he left behind
Showed what terrors can become,
When you mess with the unknown,
For the man was lying dead, stone-cold in bed.

David Merriman (13)
St Michael's School, Llanelli

THE PSORIASIS

I was walking in the forest,
On a very hubedy day,
Picking scrumptious berries,
In the same hubedly way.

At that moment while picking berries,
Came a grazeling roar,
The whole of the forest, the trees, the flowers,
Was as still as the stillish floor.

A creature landed in the forest,
With meanful, babeling eyes,
Its mouth was glubbery and slubbery,
But I try to keep still I tries.

It walked towards me with squelch and belch,
But I nowt move an inch,
My eyes, its eyes looking still as still,
But I dare not flinch.

'Tis was the evil psoriasis,
The large and roaring dragon,
With sharp, piercing claws,
Enough to tear a wagon.

It grabbed me suddenly with corrosive strength,
I couldn't move a twitch,
The pain and agony the creature gave me,
Crushing me to tiny titch.

In front of me I see a stick,
Quite strong, sharp and runt,
I reach to get the jabbed stick
And jab it with fierceful hunt.

The psoriasis screamed and cried
And released me in pain,
It flew off in the cloudy sky,
I ran back home in rain.

Abilashraj Kanapathyraja (13)
St Michael's School, Llanelli

THE THUNDER BIRD

From the sky the Thunder Bird came;
With cold blue eyes of lightning.
It's gigantic wings of thunder,
Are dangerous and frightening.

It's heart produces a current:
It's sixteen hundred volts (three phase)
But please don't stare into its eyes,
Or you shall be shocked by its gaze.

This golden magnificent bird,
That was born in ancient legend;
Has electro-static feathers
And would fry you in a second!

Many a person has suffered
At the wrath of the Thunder Bird;
But those people did not listen!
So remember what you have heard.

Joshua Lewis (13)
St Michael's School, Llanelli

The Swamp Monster!

Who will go there?
What will be found?
Walking alone,
At the dead of night
Stumbles the young traveller.

Left alone,
With the swamp nearby.
The traveller hears his heart beat
And feels the air of death.
The monster is awake!

The splash, the ripple,
The monster raises up.
He feels the terror
Of the young, poor traveller
Nearby.

A grin appears
On the ugly creature
And a shiver goes
Down the traveller's spine.
Death will soon arrive!

The traveller feels
A shadow behind him
And tries to run away
The monster jumps on top of him
And takes him to the ground!

Hend Khalik (13)
St Michael's School, Llanelli

IT CAME FROM BENEATH THE DEEP

It came from beneath the deep
And hit the surface of the sea.
Tidal wave!
A huge, blue wall of water
Crashing towards the coast
Obliterating everything in its path.
Buildings washed away,
People drowning.

With wide yellow eyes searching
For prey to destroy
And kill.
Nostrils flaring, foul breath, a giant roar.
It overshadowed everything,
It towered above all.
It was immense.

The great beast bent down
To pick up his food.
Innocent, terrorised humans
Running around madly.
The monster's huge step
Made the earth shatter
And crack. A pit emerged
Beneath the crust.

Into this huge crack fell

Everything!

Alex Powles (13)
St Michael's School, Llanelli

THE CREATURE

It stepped out from behind the tree
With its miniature paw,
Its ears aware and listening.
Its face unseen I'm sure.
Its eyes reflected the light behind
They were the size of my fist.
Out of proportion with its tiny face,
Its mouth I almost missed.
Its outside was not of feathers,
Nor of scales or of fur;
But a skin that melted into the floor,
Camouflage so pure.
Once realising I
Was not a threat to it,
It carried on in its path, dragging
Its long tail through the grit.
I've never forgotten the day
I met the tiny creature
I tried to share the wonder, but
No one believed, no child nor teacher.

Sarah Hardie (13)
St Michael's School, Llanelli

WIZPIG

Wizpig goes round at night
Looking for some food,
He'll give you a fight
If he's in a bad mood.

With three eyes and a big tail
The prey won't get away,
But if he does fail
He'll stampede the other way.

Beware the Wizpig, my son!
The jaws that bite, the claws that catch!
But don't look into the sun
Or you'll see the Gandersnatch!

Owain Davies (13)
St Michael's School, Llanelli

THE JUBJUB BIRD

'Twas a cold, stormy night
When kahwhack, the lightning struck
The Jubjub is scared tonight
Kahwhack, the lightning struck.

Its weakness is its rub, rub,
Lungo bungo is its song.
Beware of the Jubjub,
'Tis ten foot long.

Beware my son,
Oh be careful my son
The Jubjub isn't dumb
And if you get scared, run.

The Jubjub approached the tree
Lungo bungo was the sound
My son began to flee
Then it emerged from the ground.

Now the Jubjub in sight
He began to fight.
Then, kahwoo, kahwhack
The Jubjub met eternal light.

Yousuf Sabah (14)
St Michael's School, Llanelli

A MYSTERIOUS CREATURE

It flies around the high mountains,
Zigzagging between the peaks.
Gliding down like a fountain.
It can fly for weeks and weeks.

Its eyes are a bright yellow,
Not missing anything.
Its sound is not a bellow
Nor a sharp sting.

It guards its young with tender care
That only a mother can give.
If you come too close you better beware
Because the phoenix will always live.

Kate Davies (13)
St Michael's School, Llanelli

A DIGLORAK

A Diglorak is like a mole
but bigger and has more teeth
more gruesome and cruel than a hungry
tiger searching for food.

It drills underground
only comes up for food
big enough to destroy a country or two
eats 1,000 pounds of flesh to fill its belly.

People say when it wakes up
it will be hungry again
it will search for food
the humans will be the hunted.

Toby Wilkins (14)
St Michael's School, Llanelli

THEY'RE COMING

'Ssh, they're coming, now.'
'Who? What? How? Coming?'
'Things big, small, umm, a cow,
There's a noise, it's like drumming.'

'Shh, they're close,
Their feet, like a slam of a door,
Their habits are gross,
Things crunch in their jaw.'

'Beware, you'll be in for a scare
Do you hear the drumming?
Their skin is bare,
Shh, they're coming.'

Gillian Finucane (13)
St Michael's School, Llanelli

THE SPIDER

The spider is my worst fear,
Its long and furry legs
And bulging eyes to
Spot its prey with.

Scurrying along the floor.
Very fast, trying to go unnoticed
Splat!
Oh no, the spider has been trodden on!

Serves its own right!
It shouldn't have come out
That'll teach the eight-legged freaks
Not to mess with me again!

Sara Khoshbin (13)
St Michael's School, Llanelli

MY NIGHTMARE

From universe to universe
I drifted slowly and gently
And I found myself on my own in a wood
And started walking from tree to tree.

The wood was dark and thick
And I felt like the only one there.
It was like being in a woody maze
And not a breeze of air.

I came out to a clearing
Where in front of me was a cave
Which looked dark and dull like the wood itself,
To enter you would've had to be brave.

And as I neared a bit more,
Out jumped a small animal.
It had scaly, rough-like lizard skin
And it did indeed look dreadful!

I started to run, but it followed me,
It followed me out of the wood.
So I ran and ran out of the trees,
Trying to look when I could.

And as I ran, it grew,
It grew very high and not pretty.
It was nearing and nearing every second,
Then at last we got into a city.

The people just stood by and watched,
They said, 'Help yourself, you're on your own kid!'
The monster got nearer
And nearer!
And then ...

I drifted back to my universe where I was safe again.

Edward Scourfield (14)
St Michael's School, Llanelli

WHAT'S THAT?

It's big and black, what's that?
It's round, hairy and fat,
It's moved from over there where it sat,
On that mat, what's that?

Large green eyes and a tail
Its name could be Jim or Gail.
What's that?
What's that?

It's a monster I think,
With a very odd wink,
He's coming to get me, I think,
I think.

Thud, thud, bang, bang
Went his feet as he sang,
Then I saw his fang and ran
Home to another beast with a fang,
My mam!

Angharad Watts (14)
St Michael's School, Llanelli

THE PHOENIX

Violet, indigo, blue, green,
Yellow, orange and red.
Have you ever seen these colours,
Shining brightly and looking lovely?

Of course you have, in the rainbow,
But, this is something else,
This is a remarkable,
Yet legendary bird.

Have you guessed?
Here are more clues.
It can consume itself by fire
Every five hundred years.

Think that's strange?
Well, it can be reborn from its ashes,
Still looking as lovely as ever!
Want more clues?

In the mythology of ancient Egypt,
This bird represented the sun,
Which dies at night
And is reborn in the morning.

Still confused?
In early Christian tradition,
This bird was a symbol of both
Immortality and resurrection.

Give up?
This legendary bird
Is none other than the
Phoenix.

Namrata Nambiar (13)
St Michael's School, Llanelli

THE CANDERBAND

For the night t'was dark and dim,
The only one to suffer was just him.
He was the bravest all could see,
But of the age of ten was he.

He wandered into places unknown
And followed a ghastly trail of bone.
From a comrade it was a dare,
But soon found out he did not care.

After a while he found in his wake,
This terrifying monster and started to shake.
For it was the terrible canderband,
It pounced from a bush and ate his hand.

The boy let out a blood-curdling shriek,
But there was little this boy so mild and meek
Could do to fight this monster mean and big,
Into the ground his fingernails dig.

The six-foot monster showed no mercy,
As he continued swallowing Percy!
But there were few who could stop this creature,
With many a strange and absurd feature.

So this is how the story will end,
So please for me with your ears lend.
Do not go into the woods at night,
For you are sure to get a terrible fright.

Charlotte Stevens (13)
St Michael's School, Llanelli

My Nightmare

I went into bed,
Feeling so tired and dead,
I counted sheep,
Then went slowly to sleep.

I slept so quietly,
Not a sound, not a peep,
I then saw myself in a bed asleep,
And then in a desert land.

I started walking,
With no talking,
Moving pace by pace,
Then I looked and fear spread right across my face.

A huge monster
Jumped out of sight,
It grabbed my arms, it grabbed my legs,
It gave me such a fright.

It had a face, human in fact,
With eyes, a nose, a mouth and hair,
It looked at me with no care,
With wings that came to bear.

I writhed, I screamed,
The monster laughing at my struggle,
I looked closely at his face,
And then I realised it was the school bully called Race.

He picked me up,
Spread his wings and started to fly away,
I screamed, higher and higher,
I screamed so much, I awoke with fright.

I jumped up with a start,
The sweat running off my face,
Knowing that I was taken by a bully called Race,
I then realised that it was a dream,
But I could still hear my scream.

Matthew Stone (13)
St Michael's School, Llanelli

NIGHTMARE

The man looked straight at me
And I looked back.
Staring at me with those cold brown eyes
And that dead white face,
Whilst I trembled in fear.

His appearance made me want to run,
And burst into tears,
Or shrivel up in a corner.
There he waited to haunt me
Every night.

Whilst I laid in a dream,
Which turned into a nightmare,
The man came up,
Tall and frightful,
Which made me wake up with a scream.

Drenched full of sweat
As I laid on my bed,
I tried to forget,
But the nightmare went on.
Now I dread to fall asleep.

Giulia Argano (13)
St Michael's School, Llanelli

NIGHTMARE

As I slip into my dreamworld,
My peaceful journey begins,
As a beautiful land of mystery,
Filled with love and warmth of those around.

But I neglect to see with my eyes,
The darkness moving closer and closer.
As the wind begins to blow ice
In bitterly cold sweeps.

Unbearable for now my perfect world,
Not of icy cold, but riddled with flame,
Has cast upon me, like a swarm of wasps,
Burning and suffocating.

I try to run but am pulled back
By an unbearable but powerful creature,
Only describable by its eyes
Filled with evil, a reminder of pain.

They are now staring straight at me,
Looking through me,
Into my soul for a weakness,
Piercing, torturing.

I recognise those eyes.
They are of my reoccurring nightmare.
For the eyes. My fear of all fears,
They are those of death.

Claire Francis (14)
St Michael's School, Llanelli

MY WORST NIGHTMARE

I moved along the moonlit path
Frightened and hurried in the dark
When all of a sudden I heard a noise
A penetrating, trembling, awful bark.

I spun around but no one was there
I could hear the rapid beat of my heart
I quickened my pace, then started to run
To a house that was falling apart.

A high-pitched scream pierced the air
An icy shiver ran down my spine
Footsteps followed close behind me
A ghostly figure let out a whine.

I scrambled through the twisting branches
Lightning ripped the starless sky
Breathless, I stumbled into the house
And tried to scream but my throat was dry.

What stood before me I couldn't describe
A sort of monster, ten foot high
Glaring, snarling, drooling down at me
I truly thought I was going to die.

Shivering uncontrollably I woke up
My mother's eyes met my stare
I was speechless; cold sweat ran down my back
My horrifying, shocking worst nightmare.

Clare Jenkins (13)
St Michael's School, Llanelli

SPIDERS

When I see a spider,
My mouth drops wider.

When I see one scuttle across the floor,
I find myself unable to move anymore.

When I see one hanging from the ceiling,
I get the most horrible feeling.

'But sometimes I'm not that bothered,' I said,
'But of course that's only when I see them dead.'

Stephanie Whitlow (13)
St Michael's School, Llanelli

THE MYSTERIOUS CREATURE IN THE DARK

I saw the creature in the night
Glaring at me, though in fright.
It shot a stare, with eyes clenched tight
I blinked and it swooped out of sight.

I saw it hide behind a tree
I knew its eyes were watching me
I searched but I just couldn't see
At that second I had to flee.

Emily Donoghue (13)
St Michael's School, Llanelli

DISCRIMINATION

D ark my colour is,
I llegal discrimination is,
S mall my size is,
C ymraeg my language is,
R oman Catholic my religion is,
I llegal discrimination is,
M iddle-class my parents are,
I llegal discrimination is,
N ormal does not exist,
A sian my family is,
T ubby my body is,
I llegal discrimination is,
O ld my age is,
N ormal cannot exist.

Jack Bamber (13)
Sir Thomas Picton School

PREJUDICE

P ulled away from the world
R eligion was the same
E veryone hated us just 'cause of our colour
J umping round at night, waiting for us to come
U ntil the morning sun
D anger lurked every day
I nstead we hid in fear
C aught in a world, we were trapped
E verybody hated us just 'cause we were black.

Alice Tucker (13)
Sir Thomas Picton School

DISCRIMINATION

D ispleasure surges into the heart of those who are discriminated
   against,
I ntense remarks that hurt and cause a person to bleed inside,
S arcastic comments that may ruin an honourable person's reputation,
C ries of pain from the poor victim of discrimination,
R eputations put at stake by statements that discriminate,
I nnocent bystanders are drawn into the fight that is discrimination,
M emories of harsh discrimination acts cannot fade,
I diotic comments from narrow-minded people add to the fray,
N asty and unfeeling, although many people do not realise it,
A ctions that are unkind and unjust may be one form of discrimination,
T easing, taunting and traumatising are three words to describe
   discrimination,
I ncessant gossip about 'who did what' and 'where',
O ften people are discriminated against because of their race
   or religion,
N othing helps to soothe the pain of one that has suffered
   from discrimination.

Danielle Cristofaro (13)
Sir Thomas Picton School

RAP O' RACIAL DISCRIMINATION

Racial discrimination is not the way ahead,
Wit' some people lyin' safer in their beds.
White boy, black boy, one big swirl,
An on-going feud all over the world . . .

Fights an' battles, mobs an' wars,
Blood is spilt in the name of t' Lord.
Friends torn apart, families took away,
All in the hope of a bran' new day . . .

But what is all this fightin' really for?
The wars don't stop, an' there will be more.
Why don't they finish an' call it quits?
They know all the worl' will fall into bits.

The races are dyin', the religion is lost,
Now people can't just go to a mosque.
Bombs an' timers, knives an' guns,
Can't they see this will never be won?

Tom Staniford (13)
Sir Thomas Picton School

DISCRIMINATION

D espised by the human race,
I gnorant too, that's what they are.
S corned and scoffed at by everyone.
C lassed as inferior.
R ejected for things because of it.
I mmoral acts.
M ocked and jeered at.
I solated from the rest of mankind.
N ever will I be able to sleep soundly in my bed.
A bused for being black.
T aunted, but I just walk past.
I nsults thrown at me every day.
O ppressed just like slaves long ago.
N arrow-minded instead of big-hearted.

Melanie Thomas (13)
Sir Thomas Picton School

I'M BLACK

Stripped of my freedom,
Afraid of the outside world,
Discriminated,
Why?
My colour

Isolated in the darkness,
Coldly cast aside,
Discriminated,
Why?
My colour

I scream for justice and
Pray for a better life,
Discriminated,
Why?
My colour

Skin should not matter,
It's the person you are,
Discriminated,
Why?
My colour

Is it not possible to live
In harmony with each other?
I guess not,
So I'll always be
Discriminated,
Why?
I'm black.

Libby Matthews (13)
Sir Thomas Picton School

FACES IN THE STREET

Just yesterday,
Well really, all my life,
As I walk down the street,
Every day is the same.

I tower above all else,
With my short black hair,
Crystal teeth
And ivory fingernails.

It's like being shut off
From the rest of the world.

Even in the middle of a bustling street,
I'm so alone,
It used to make me angry,
But all I feel now is sadness and pain.

When children walk past me
And even sometimes adults
Who should know better,
They glare wide-eyed at me
Like I'm some sort of freak show.

It gets much worse,
Sniggering and whispering,
And people throw things at you,
It's like being treated as an animal.

One day I wish
Someone would say,
He's just a person,
Just like you,
Just like me.

Laura Morgan (13)
Sir Thomas Picton School

WHY?

All you need is love.
Some people would disagree,
White, black, it's all the same to

                    Me.

Some people have decided,
Hastily, I agree
We should not judge others so

                    Unknowingly.

There is no excuse for prejudice.
For you, or for me,
To have a fixed opinion

            And not to
               Wait and see.

It doesn't matter if you're black or white
Just you wait and see
How we all judge each other,

                    Carelessly.

Some open up to others, well
Without even using a key
But for some to do, maybe me or you

                    This is not so easy.

Why can't we all get along?
Because, because, because . . .
Does anyone have the answer
For why we are so prejudice?

Anita Mattson (14)
Sir Thomas Picton School

IT'S ONLY A COLOUR

D oes it matter if you're black or white?
I t's only a colour.
S houldn't be called names or bullied because of it. It's only a
C olour.
R acist abuse from
I gnorant people.
M akes me feel insecure and unwanted.
I don't understand, it's only a colour.
N ever do people laugh with me, only
A t me.
T hey talk about me, whisper things when I walk in the room.
I t's only a colour.
O nlookers see my pain.
N obody helps me.

Jane Thomas (13)
Sir Thomas Picton School

PREJUDICE

P eople hate me, but they have no
R eason. They do not know me but still I am disliked.
E lderly and young are all discriminated against,
J ust for their colour. The difference between black and white is
U nknown. The comments always hurt, but I put up with them
D espite the pain I feel
I nside. There is always whispering, pointing and then the
C ruel laughter. But for me that's life, and it will be until blacks
   and whites are
E qual.

Bethan Hayes (13)
Sir Thomas Picton School

DISCRIMINATION AT ITS BEST

Isolated from the rest of the world,
Yes, I'm black, I have been told.
Why do you look at me in that awful way?
Maybe you can't at night but you can in day.

You beat me up, black and blue,
H-hey, don't turn your b-back, I'm talking to you.
Look, you walk away like I don't mean anything,
If you get to know me, you may see something.

Think, why does everyone criticise me? Because I'm a different colour,
You're blue when you're cold, yellow when ill and white all over.
Everybody! Do you know I'm not an animal?
In the mind you compare me to a tribe of cannibals.

Just because you're a little bit different,
People don't have to hibernate in their own homes,
You all do have movement.
Come on everyone let's join together,
And win this war that's been going on forever and ever.

Nick Faichney (13)
Sir Thomas Picton School

DISCRIMINATION

Colour's just a colour,
Pink, green, blue,
But when it comes to black and white,
That will never do.

They curse you in the daytime,
They hunt you in the night,
And for what awful purpose?
Simply because they're white.

Cold as a snowflake,
Hard as iron bars,
Yet even though they ridicule,
They taunt you from *afar*.

When you think of night-time,
The milky moon is bright,
Before the shadow curtain,
Ignore the black, because there's white.

Stephanie Johns (13)
Sir Thomas Picton School

DISCRIMINATION

What does it matter
That someone's skin is a few shades darker?
Why should it affect
What school they attend
Or job they can get?

Is it really worth
The cost of people's lives
Because people can't agree whether a person should
Worship in a mosque or synagogue?
Sometimes we have to account
For other people's beliefs
To make a bit of world peace

When I look around the place
I think that Earth would be a bit boring
If everyone was the same religion or race.

Eva Hannah (14)
Sir Thomas Picton School

DISCRIMINATION

D eserted by the outside world
I nferior to other races
S abotaged by harsh white tongues
C riticised for our coloured faces
R ejected from all social life
I gnominious comments in the streets
M arked a freak, that's what I am
I might as well admit defeat
N ot a day goes by without some kind of bullying
A gainst my race, my culture, and my coloured skin
T aunted by people who think I'm different
I gnorant are the ones who commit this sin, but
O ver the years you might have noticed
N ot one black person has *ever* given in.

Kayleigh Morris (13)
Sir Thomas Picton School

QUANTITY NOT QUALITY!

He sits on his chair all day long,
Not caring if he is right or wrong,
He hears a one-sided tale from his mate,
For more information he won't wait.

He'll discriminate the latest person
For their religion or race he'll keep on cursing,
For people less fortunate he feels no pain,
All he thinks of is personal gain.

He doesn't like his job because he is lazy,
His boss and his workmates are going crazy,
They're getting annoyed with what he thinks,
He's so opinionated it really stinks.

He is rude and arrogant to all he sees,
He thinks he's the best, the bee's knees,
He always has a lot to say,
Quantity not quality, that's his way.

Bertie Brown (13)
Sir Thomas Picton School

DISCRIMINATION

D   iscrimination has a bad meaning.
I   t's the inside that counts.
S   ociety in general does discriminate.
C   olour of skin.
R   eligious beliefs can cause wars.
I   mpossible to change everyone's views.
M   ixed marriages cause problems.
I   t should be dealt with.
N   ew laws can help fight discrimination.
A   ttitudes are changing.
T   eaching the young can help change things.
I   gnorance can be a cause.
O   lder generation.
N   eed to educate.

Kimberley Doncaster (13)
Sir Thomas Picton School

DISCRIMINATION

D arker skin
I gnored by white
S hut out from society
C ursed by 'lights'
R un around in circles
I lliterately blind
M auled by jaws of snapping whites
I njured by words that fill my plate
N othing to help me stop this fight
A lone to suffer
T errified by 'light'
I ndifferent I am
O nly colour not the same
N othing will stop me being like whites.

Michael Christopher (13)
Sir Thomas Picton School

DISCRIMINATION

If a Brit is white,
And a Spaniard is tanned,
Whereas an Italian is olive,
Why is an Indian 'coloured'?

If they can't sing,
And he can't act,
Whereas she can't dance,
Why am I called 'disabled'?

If a brunette is a brunette,
And a redhead is a redhead,
Whereas dark hair is dark hair,
Why is a blonde 'a bimbo'?

If a Jew is a Jew,
And a Christian is a Christian,
Whereas a Hindu is a Hindu,
Why is a Muslim 'a Paki'?

Ishita Ranjan (13)
Sir Thomas Picton School

DISCRIMINATION

D iscriminated because
I 'm black.
S o annoyed to be
C alled names because of my colour.
R ejected from normal life,
I 'm ignored by
M ean, unfair, horrible people.
I magine all the pain and fear.
N ot being thought of as a normal person,
A lthough I try to ignore it, I'm
T reated unfairly.
I t's like being locked in a cage
O n my own
N owhere to go, no one I know.

Alex Lewis (13)
Sir Thomas Picton School

DISCRIMINATION

Protected by law,
But it is still a flaw.
You think we are different,
Which is due to my colour.

You would be different,
If you came to my home.
We hate you and you wonder why?
You treat us like dirt,
Just because our skin is the same colour.

You think we are different,
And sometimes we agree,
We think this way,
Because you treat us this way.
All we want is a life, a life which we can use.
To be able to read or write
But to you this is not right.
Oh please give us a chance,
We could do what jobs you do,
Or are you frightened of us,
For we might be better or cleverer than you?

Let us be equal,
Let us be free,
There's not much difference
Between you and me.

Jack Pinson (14)
Sir Thomas Picton School

RACISM

Always treated bad, criticised and despised
It makes me feel awfully sad
I'm not all that bad

Tears run down my face
I need some friends
Don't want to be alone in this place

We are the ones always put last
Me, my family
They don't know our past

I want to stop this now
All these horrible, nasty rows
Wars, guns, bombs, all sorts
All the tears shed

I cry, I pray every day
That we shall have peace some day
We are just crying for help

You hurt our feelings
Make us sad
I mean it, we are not all that bad
We are all the human race
Just a different colour
And a different face.

Charlie Anne Smith (13)
Sir Thomas Picton School

LOVE IS SUCH A CRAZY THING

People say I'm crazy
People say I'm lazy
Don't understand love
Don't know how to feel
Don't know if it is real
Can't have a relationship
It always ends up in the tip
I just know
I have to let you go
Before we go too deep
Wanna sunbathe on the beach
Don't wanna end up on the street
Listening to the same old beat
I buy my own rings
Love is such a crazy thing
I've had a rough ride
I've had a crazy life
Nobody came along to open up my mind
You've got to understand my side
Because I'm so young
I'm not ready to open up.

James Woodridge (16)
Tregynon Hall School

MY MUM AND I

I love my mum, she is good fun
living without her makes me feel glum.
When we're apart, it breaks my heart
when we're together, I wish it was forever.
At this moment in time, we get along just fine
unlike the past, I know it will last.

I knew it wasn't right when we used to fight,
Mother and I used to shout at each other,
now everything's all right, we get along just fine.
I've been at the school over a year
I miss my mum, but I cope with the fears
The school is cool, so I never act the fool.
So that's why I am at Tregynon Hall School.

Sarah Jane Reynolds (14)
Tregynon Hall School

FOOTBALL

Football is about eleven men chasing a ball
Until the ref gives a call.
The ball is white, it flies like a kite
When you score it's a wonderful sight
Fouls are sad when they're bad,
But when you play it's a great day.
Football is a way of life, it's better than
Having a wife.
Football is a game of two halves,
Some you win, some you lose, either way
You have to choose.
Win, win, win - lose, lose, lose,
It's up to you, what you do.
Just don't stand and gas,
Get the ball and pass.
A team of players who play together
Is a recipe for success and you'll
never get less.

Mark Jones (13)
Tregynon Hall School

A SPANISH HOLIDAY POEM

Not worried, but excited
standing on deck, waving goodbye.
The ferry, huge and bold
when we went on,
it rocked and rolled as we went by.
We scoured the sea for
dolphins and other friendly creatures.
We went to restaurants and cafés
to eat and drink on the way to Spain -
but French waitresses, how very odd!
And when it was disco time, we danced
and sang with happy smiles.

The time seemed to go slower
than in England, but we continually
went back and forth to the map to see
how far we had gone.
Surrounded by blue and white clouds,
adrift in the world, about to begin
the adventure.

Robert Campbell (14)
Tregynon Hall School

A FEAR

I have a fear
Not a fear of a child
Like a monster roaring taunts
Or any of that nature
It is not those that haunt

It is not horror
Like Children of the Corn
Nothing of that sort
Not even like the spike upon the Devil's horn

Night by night
Waiting to see if near
That droning sound of what
It's not the wind, I hear

I'm living this out
The fear I dare
My fear is war that's the word I swear.

Oliver Brian Lambert (14)
Tregynon Hall School

THE STORM

There is a storm outside
brewing like beer in a barrel.
Clouds are gathering, like milk
when poured into tea.
Rain falling like cries of
happiness, the sound of thunder
in the sky, crashing and banging
like wind chimes in a storm.

The lightning crackling,
clashes blinding as their
lights flash at me.
The wind wheels like the call
of a farmer's whistle calling
his dog . . . and so the rain
carried on and on, as the rain
made a tune all through
the night. The storm carried on.

Adam Rushton (13)
Tregynon Hall School

THAT WORD

What? . . . What was that word?
Ever since I heard that word I freeze whenever anyone says it.
My muscles clench, I cannot move for a few seconds.

It scares me, it must scare others.
I curse that word ever since I heard and found out what it means.

It's like a black misted hand that grabs your body.
It doesn't let go, it just lingers, shutting you down.

Rarely we get it to let go, but mostly we can do nothing, it won't let go.
We have to watch, we feel dumbstruck.
We feel helpless.
We cry, we weep.
Month upon month we sit cherishing every moment.

That spiteful feeling inside wants to drive us into the ground.
We don't want to let go.
That evil hand has grabbed them.
We say goodbye.
We weep.
We cry.

For days and days we sit in mourning.
Slowly, slowly going down.
Because it's won, that evil hand has won.
That evil word we call
Cancer.

James Brennan (14)
Tregynon Hall School

SORROW

A gathering of black
A coffin being lowered
A peaceful beauty asleep within
She shouldn't be in there
She's too young and small to die
The silence took her
And never was she to
Cry and sigh again
Never to see her
Wild free eyes again
And never was I to see her smile again.

Rose Lilliman (15)
Tregynon Hall School

CONFUSED

C   onfused - is like having an overloaded fuse for a brain
O   nly fuzzing in your head, nothing works
N   ot on task, that's what the teacher says
F   rustrated, can't do anything
U   seless, it's like banging your head against a brick wall.
S   o confused, nothing to focus on
E   ndless confusion
D   arting from subject to subject
            I am confused.

David Mitchell (14)
Tregynon Hall School

SEASONS

Seasons come and seasons go
Some pass quickly,
And some pass slow.

Some are cold and some are hot,
Some are bright and some are not.

In spring the weather is bright and breezy,
In summer the children feel all queasy,
In autumn the leaves fall off the trees
When winter comes, we cough and sneeze.

Some are cold and some are hot,
Some are bright and some are not.

In spring the flowers peep through the ground,
In summer the children gather around,
In autumn the trees are bare,
Go out in winter, if you dare!

Cathleen Lloyd (12)
Ysgol Gyfun Emlyn

AMORE

I sit alone, meal for two.
I'm only one, can I join you?
I've been alone, most of my life.
I want a friend, not a wife.

A candle burns with my desire,
My heart, it yearns within the fire
Love that's flammable, but doesn't light
For you, I waited, all last night.

I cannot wait, my clock, it chimes!
My love has been dampened, many times.
Faces will pass me by, I'm sure,
But it's only for you I feel amore.

Stephanie Goodeve (14)
Ysgol Gyfun Emlyn

WUTHERING HEIGHTS

Passionate crying I can hear,
And gentle little rumbles
From the dark, overcast sky.
A handsome young man, sauntering
Across moors with inclining rage,
As the thunder and the persevering wind
Moans and howls.

He doesn't notice the almighty crack
As the bough of a tree causes the chimney stack to fall.
Someone is on their knees, supplicating the Lord
And a young woman, inundate from the rain
Is refusing to take shelter.
She is worried for the handsome man
No longer in her sight.

As it approaches half-past midnight
The saturated woman is bid to bed.
The crying has halted, the delinquent asleep
And the intentional young woman
Begged to remove her wet things
Admits herself to bed.
Silence fell, as Wuthering Heights slept.

Emma Lynch (15)
Ysgol Gyfun Emlyn

OLD JIP

Old Jip, he was a farm dog,
Who led a busy life,
His master's friend was he,
Through happiness and strife.

His master's sheep were in his keep,
He never let them roam,
Through wind and rain he drove them,
And brought them safely home.

One cold and frosty morning,
Jip was not at the gate,
His master went to find out why,
His faithful friend was late.

Jip was lying, cold and still,
His life was at an end.
'What will I do,' the farmer cried,
'Without my faithful friend!'

Luke Evetts (14)
Ysgol Gyfun Emlyn

DISAPPEARED

A girl looks out of the open window
Clutching her teddy bear tight
The wind is blowing, the birds are singing
The sun is shining bright.

As I stare at her smiling face
She has no care in the world
But look harder beneath that gentle smile
She dare not say a word.

I watch her carefully and then I see
This tiny little tear
She looks slowly at her bent photographs
Of her family that have disappeared.

Amy Lynch (13)
Ysgol Gyfun Emlyn

THE GODDESS OF THE NIGHT

She passes through the mist and fog,
She lingers through the land.
She shadows all beneath her feet
And darkens with her hand.

She passes over sea and land
And mountains in the sky.
She passes over desert hot,
But does not rest nor die.

She brings fear to those who cannot sleep,
She carries demons, dark and deep.
She does not stop till all is gone
And buried till the morning come.

She fears the sun, who comes by day
And spreads her light around.
She fades away as dawn begins
And hides beneath the ground.

She holds the stars within her soul,
The moon within her heart.
And as the dusk comes slowly round,
She tears the light apart.

Isobel Lawrence (14)
Ysgol Gyfun Emlyn

THE BEST ONE?

You'd never have guessed it,
You'd never have known,
That she'd be the best one in the whole home.
She has blonde, curly hair,
Right down to her knees,
She looks so angelic, that you wouldn't believe.
She lives with cats,
Big and small
And herself, she is quite, quite tall.
Her dress is terror black,
Her coat is blood-red
And her tights, of course, are the colour of the dead.
The other one's are short,
Much different to her
And they could not cast a spell, for a cat's purr.
Her name is Star,
Her eyes are red,
She'd easily just wink to wake up the dead.
She does spells,
They are long and short
And some are made-up and some are bought.
You'd never have guessed it,
You'd never have known,
That she'd be the best *witch* in the whole home!

Jessica Fogden (12)
Ysgol Gyfun Emlyn

I'M SURE MY MUM'S A HIPPY!

I'm sure my mum's a hippy,
She always wears so much lippy,
I'm sure my mum's a hippy,
The way she dresses an' all,
I'm sure my mum's a hippy,
Cos she dances so weirdly,

I'm sure my mum's a hippy,
The way she lives alone,
I'm sure my mum's a hippy,
But I still love her to pieces,
And I'm still positively sure,
My mum's a hippy!

Theresa Hillyard (12)
Ysgol Gyfun Emlyn

THE LEOPARD IN THE NIGHT

A leopard waited all night
Until it came upon a sight
In the dark
He spotted a lark.

The leopard hadn't eaten for days
He had tried different tactics and ways
The bird's life he had to steal
In order to get this easy meal.

He leaped and pounced
For his hunting skills were renounced
Lately he had bad luck
And his hunting skills were beginning to suck.

He gathered his courage and became bold
He got his prey and struck pure gold.

Andrew Smith (12)
Ysgol Gyfun Emlyn

THE PATHWAY TO WUTHERING HEIGHTS

The path goes winding ever onwards.
The frost shattered peaks,
The high mountain mist,
The path goes winding ever onwards.

Into the steep-sided valleys,
Through the wooded slopes,
The mountain peaks hiding in their mist.
The path goes winding ever onwards.

The clear and fresh mountain springs,
They fall into the black lakes below.
Turning round the heather filled moors,
The path goes winding ever onwards.

And to Wuthering Heights it goes,
That dark and brooding house,
That ruined world where Heathcliffe lurks.
The path goes winding ever onwards.

John Newman (14)
Ysgol Gyfun Emlyn

I'M SURE MY DAD'S AN APE!

I'm sure my dad's an ape
his belly is all covered in hair!
I'm sure my dad's an ape
his arms could stretch around the world!
I'm sure my dad's an ape
he never talks sense!
I'm sure my dad's an ape
his hair grows so quickly!

I'm sure my dad's an ape
he always makes weird noises!
I'm sure my dad's an ape
he's never, ever responsible
Guess what?
I'm sure my dad's an *ape!*

India Latter (12)
Ysgol Gyfun Emlyn

WUTHERING HEIGHTS

All the days are fast and fun,
Endless places to play and run,
The nights bring darkness and the cold,
Two children hold hands they're getting old.

Time passes quicker each and every day,
Hearts are broken people don't stay,
Love is now nowhere to be seen,
They imagine what it could have been.

Logs thrown on dying fires,
Trying to block out the endless lies,
Feelings all mixed up with the weather,
The chilling moors rolling with heather.

Everything seems silent and dead,
All have left an empty bed,
The sheets are strewn across the floor,
The wind blows back the broken door.

Gemma Conway (15)
Ysgol Gyfun Emlyn

Was It Me?

The wheels roll,
Smoothly, swish,
The puck glides,
Hit from a stick,
I take it,
Shoot,
Goal!
The wheels roll,
Smoothly, swish,
Eagle eyes,
Referee,
The whistle blows,
Was it me?
The wheels roll,
Smoothly, swish.

David Beckingsale (12)
Ysgol Gyfun Emlyn

Conker Day

The scene was set
In the playground
No room to let
In the surround.

The place was filled
Of amateurs
All playing games
With their conkers.

There were big ones
There were small ones
They cracked
And smacked.

They crashed
And smashed
Falling to the ground
And silence fell, all over the playground.

Charlie Jackson (12)
Ysgol Gyfun Emlyn

MEMORY IN A SHOE

Shoes come in different sizes
small, large, medium
shoes come in different colours
red, yellow, blue, green, orange, black
shoes come in different designs
shoes come in boxes
shoes become old
shoes are new
shoes have memories
old and new
I remember my shoes
black with frilly laces
big and bulky
and came in a box
I had them for two years
and what a wild time I had
in my black shoes with frilly laces.

Stuart Smith (15)
Ysgol Rhydygors

TYRES

Tyres are big
tyres are small
tyres can come
any size or form
big ones, small ones,
thick ones, thin ones
any colour you choose
delivered to your door
black, blue, piles of them
waiting to be bought
shiny and smelling of rubber
I wish I had a car
to buy a set of new tyres.

Nicholas Herbert (13)
Ysgol Rhydygors

COURAGE

Some people call me names
Some people kick and punch me
I don't like to show it
Otherwise they will think they have hurt me

They're just big bullies who like to hurt little kiddies
But when they are confronted, they are just little teddies
I'm a strong person who never gives us fighting
So if you're being bullied, do the same as I did.
Ignore them.

Clive O'Connor (13)
Ysgol Rhydygors

DOLPHINS

Early in the evening as the
moon is rising, see the
little dolphins
swimming along
and the stars are glittering
beyond the shiny sea and
they are as beautiful
as your dreams can be.

Dolphins leaping high
trying to touch the moon
as memorable as seeing
a shooting star outside my
bedroom.

John James (15)
Ysgol Rhydygors